W. J. Cunningham

10ª

Underlined

Well-Known
Memphis Pastor

Author Famous, too!

WHOM
CHRIST
COMMENDED

WHOM
CHRIST
COMMENDED

Ralph W. Sockman

ABINGDON PRESS   NEW YORK • NASHVILLE

WHOM CHRIST COMMENDED

Copyright © 1963 by Abingdon Press

Library of Congress Catalog Card Number: 63-11381

SET UP, PRINTED, AND BOUND BY
THE PARTHENON PRESS, AT NASHVILLE,
TENNESSEE, UNITED STATES OF AMERICA

Dedicated to my sister
Ethel Sockman Barre

PREFACE

This book has been twenty years growing above ground. The seed was planted in my mind by my friend Jacob Payton, who was long connected with *The Christian Advocate*. He said that religion is so often thought of in terms of warnings and rebukes. "Why not write about the compliments Christ paid?"

In reading the Gospels I find only nine clearly recorded cases of explicit praise paid by Jesus to specific individuals. One of these is to his disciples as a group. There were no doubt many, many more words of commendation spoken by the Christ, which the Gospels fail to report.

Yet these rare recorded situations serve to reveal Jesus' principle of cultivation by encouragement. In describing his mission, he said, "God sent the Son into the world, not to condemn the world, but that the world might be saved through him." (John 3:17.) Paul caught the spirit of Christ when he said, not only "by grace you have been saved through faith" (Eph. 2:8), but also, "In this hope we were saved" (Romans 8:24).

Jesus did not hesitate to condemn wrongdoing in scathing terms. But while he humbled sinners, he did not humiliate them. He left them looking up. He sought to bring out the best in people by showing that he expected the best of them.

On the other hand Jesus did not gloss over the defects in all those he commended. He pinpointed their virtues without erasing their errors. He praised Nicodemus and John the Baptist, but neither became apostles.

7

These brief chapters will no doubt raise questions which will send the reader seeking for further answers. Why did Jesus see in the Roman centurion, with the sick slave, a faith such as he had not found in all Israel? (Luke 7:9.) What is the full implication of Jesus' tribute to Zacchaeus: "Today salvation has come to this house, since he also is a son of Abraham?" (Luke 19:9). Was the publican's disgorging of his dishonest gains enough to save him?

It is my hope that these portrayals will lead the reader to look more deeply into the situations. So many who studied my latest book, *The Meaning of Suffering,* have asked me to write another set of biblical studies for group use. Maybe some will find this volume suitable for such a purpose.

To thank all who have aided me by sharing their thoughts would be impossible. May I single out the following: Miss Juliet Endly, Miss Fanny Alliger, and Mrs. W. C. Stevens, for valuable research; Miss Geneva Helm, my sermon and radio secretary, for advice and secretarial services; and my wife, Zellah Endly Sockman, for her continued counsel and insight through the years.

RALPH W. SOCKMAN

January, 1963

CONTENTS

I. FAITH OF THE FIRST GRADE

How do we grade the quality of faith? If "faith is the assurance of things hoped for, the conviction of things not seen," is it to be graded according to the height of its hopes and the extent of its expectations? For instance, if I believe that God will soon bring Russia and America into brotherly comradeship, is my faith of higher grade than that of the person who expects only that the two nations will coexist without a nuclear war?

Or is faith to be rated according to the confidence one puts into his convictions? For example, if you believe so strongly in God's power to heal that you trust your illness to his cure without other aid, while I will call in medical help, is yours a higher and finer faith than mine?

This is no mere academic question, because we live by faith and we are "saved by faith." A child breathes the atmosphere of faith in the home, for only by faith can people dwell together in families. By faith we ride to work and plan tomorrow's program. Faith is the working principle of life, manifest in the tiny tot crossing the street with her hand in her mother's or in a Columbus crossing the Atlantic when his only chart "was one which faith deciphered in the skies." Robert Louis Stevenson was right when he said that faith forms the axles of the universe.

The Gospels of Matthew and Luke record the case of a Roman centurion to whom Jesus gave a grade *A* for faith. There are slight divergencies in the two accounts. In Matthew's record, "As he entered

Capernaum a centurion came forward to him, beseeching him and saying, 'Lord, my servant is lying paralyzed at home in terrible distress." Jesus replied, "I will come and heal him." But the centurion demurred at taking Jesus to his home, saying, "Lord I am not worthy to have you come under my roof."

Luke paints the centurion's humility in even stronger colors.

He reports that the Roman officer sent some Jewish elders to Jesus with the plea. The elders besought Jesus earnestly, saying of the centurion, "He is worthy to have you do this for him, for he loves our nation, and he built us our synagogue." Jesus went with them. When he was not far from the house, the centurion sent friends to the Master saying:

"Lord, do not trouble yourself, for I am not worthy to have you come under my roof; therefore I did not presume to come to you. But say the word and let my servant be healed. For I am a man set under authority, with soldiers under me; and I say to one, 'Go,' and he goes; and to another, 'Come,' and he comes; and to my slave, 'Do this,' and he does it." When Jesus heard this he marveled at him, and turned and said to the multitude that followed him, "I tell you, not even in Israel have I found such faith."

Matthew also reports Jesus as making to those who accompanied him a statement which expresses his admiration for the faith of the Roman centurion in contrast to the lack of faith shown by his own fellow Israelites. Unquestionably the Gospels record this incident of the centurion to show that Jesus awakened the faith of the Gentiles quite as much as that of the Israelites, and sometimes even more. No doubt Jesus' commendation of the centurion's faith partly derived from the fact that it came from such an unexpected source.

It seems noteworthy that the Revised Standard Version translates Jesus as saying, "Not even in Israel have I found such faith," whereas the King James Version puts it "so great faith." It was not the greatness or extent of the centurion's faith which was so significant. It was the pure quality of it. Here we are seeing faith at its pure source before it becomes complicated by doctrinal beliefs or muddied by ceremonialism.

In 1953 we visited the city of Benares, India. I had read some of the beautiful sayings of the Hindu mystics and had heard the appealing interpretations of certain distinguished Hindu philosophers. But at Benares we saw the people manifesting their faith in daily practice. We looked into temple rooms where tables were laden with food for their idols. We were not allowed to enter, but sacred cows could push past us and walk among the tables of viands. In the courtyard of the temple we came upon a low mound of clotted blood surrounding a stake where animals were sacrificed. Poor, trusting people believed that the blood of those animals smeared on their bodies had some mystic power to appease their deity. It is not much wonder that many thoughtful people dismiss religion as mere superstition when they think of the meaningless things done in its name, yes, even by Christians.

After our return from India I went to call on a highly educated member of my church, the late Joseph E. Goodbar, who had for months been lying stricken with a baffling disease. His physical eyes had grown dim, but his spiritual vision had been sharpened by pain and prayer. I discussed with him the question, "Where Faith Begins," which was the sermon theme for the following Sunday. He said something like this: "As I see it, the kernel of our faith is in the old words of the prophet Micah: 'What does the Lord require of you but to do justice, and to love kindness, and to walk humbly with your God?'"

At the time the prophet Micah wrote those words, his people were trying to appease Jehovah with their sacrificial offerings of rams and bullocks, olive oil and grains. Their ceremonials became ever more elaborate, but their religious faith was divorced from their character. And Micah cried:

> Will the Lord be pleased with thousands of rams,
> with ten thousands of rivers of oil?

No, what Jehovah wants from us is justice, kindness, humble godliness.

The essential of religious faith is trustworthy character, and no amount of ceremonies can be a substitute. Micah saw that in his day; Jesus saw it in his. The Roman centurion did not give himself to the temple ceremonies. He was not a Jew. He was a foreigner. But he had the essentials of noble character: to do justice, to love kindness, and to walk humbly with God.

Here then we note the first element in the faith Christ was commending.

As we read between the lines of the gospel record, we get a glimpse of the centurion's personality. He was kind to his servants. We can be pretty sure he was concerned about his slave as a person and not about his value as property, for slaves were undoubtedly cheap for Roman officers. The centurion was also humane in his attitude toward the people he was policing. Although not a Jew, he had respect for Jewish customs. He went further, and was generous. The Jewish elders said he had built them a synagogue. He apparently possessed the qualities which earned the respect of people across national and class and religious lines.

In short, the centurion was a person in whom others could put faith. This is a basic but often overlooked point in our consideration of faith. Faith is a working principle of daily living and not merely a sixth sense by which we apprehend realities for which we have no other evidence. Many think that when we talk about religious faith we are leaving the solid ground of reality for a realm of speculation and make-believe. They assume that faith is a sort of prop for weak minds and a substitute for logic. They may even second the sneering remark of Madame de Staël: "Have you not observed that faith is generally strongest in those whose character may be called the weakest?"

Not so. Faith, to be sure, is "the conviction of things not seen." It does outrun our physical sight. But the trustworthy intuitions and insights of a person's faith derive from the trustworthiness of his character.

A successful teacher of religion in a midwestern university writes that in one period of his life he lapsed into atheism for several years. His return to faith started when he put to himself this question, "Will I do an honest day's work for an honest day's pay?" By recovering a responsible attitude toward his work, he began to clear his thoughts and to find divine meaning for his life. Integrity in one's work is one of the best ways of integrating a disturbed and doubting mind.

What we do directs our thinking as truly as what we think directs our doing. One of the nineteenth century's greatest preachers was F. W. Robertson of Brighton, England. He went through a period of doubt and depression. But he wrote a classic sermon with the title, "Obedience, the Organ of Spiritual Knowledge." It was based on Jesus' words to those who doubted his divinity. Jesus said: "If any man's will is to do his [God's] will, he shall know whether the [my] teaching is from God or whether I am speaking on my own authority." When we obey God's will to the best of our knowledge, our minds are guided toward the truth.

In the darkness of his own doubts Robertson kept saying to himself that it is better to be honest than dishonest, better to be chaste than licentious, better to be forgiving than bitter. And he came through testifying that anyone in the fog of doubt will find faith by trusting to the landmarks of morality.

So much of the contemporary writing about faith gives the impression that its main ingredient is confident expectation. If you believe confidently enough, you can have anything you want, from the winning of your next game to the presidency of your company. But if we read the Scriptures far enough to catch the whole gospel, we shall see that to have faith in God, we must be the kind of persons in whom God can have faith. It is not enough merely to *have* faith; we must *keep* faith.

Consider the parable of the talents, which is so often cited to show how faith makes for success. The man with ten talents had the faith to put them into circulation and thus gained ten more, while the cautious fellow who was afraid to invest buried his talent and lost it. The moral commonly drawn is that thus confident expectation wins and lack of confidence loses.

But read the parable again. Listen to what was said to the man of ten talents: "Well done, good and faithful servant; you have been faithful over a little. I will set you over much; enter into the joy of your master." It was not merely faith in the sense of confidence which Jesus was commending in that parable, but also—and perhaps primarily—it was faith in the sense of trustworthiness. The winners were those whom God could trust because they had proved themselves faithful to their tasks.

We are counting too much on faith without faithfulness. We should count on God, but we must first be the kind of person on whom God can count. Recall the occasion recorded by the Fourth Gospel: "Now when he was in Jerusalem at the Passover feast, many believed in his name when they saw his signs which he did; but Jesus did not trust himself to them." The centurion was of such reliable character that Jesus could put trust in him.

Secondly, note his *humility*. Despite his good record and the tribute paid him by the Jewish elders for his generosity in building them a synagogue, the centurion said to Jesus, "I am not worthy to have you come under my roof." He was sensitive to the feelings and faith of the Jews. He was aware that a Jew was not supposed to enter a Gentile home.

Humility is an essential element in faith at its source. It keeps the effort of believing from being blocked by pride of mind and heart. Like Paul, the man of faith feels that he has not yet attained, but is pressing on toward the mark of his high calling. Humility keeps the mind open to new revelation of truth.

Oliver Cromwell's crusading vigor might lead us to think of his iron will and rugged force rather than of his humble seeking of truth, but in his letter to the General Assembly of the Church of Scotland in 1650, he wrote: "I beseech you, in the bowels of Christ, think it possible that you may be mistaken." Such a spirit keeps a person from the stubbornness of the closed mind, from the short-sightedness of the cocksure, from the intolerance of the fanatic.

It is humility which helps to develop knowledge into wisdom as well as into true faith. Knowledge is the accumulation of facts; wisdom is the awareness of the more beyond the border of what has been found. Knowledge is proud that it knows so much; wisdom is humble that it knows no more.

Moreover, the humility essential to faith must be of the *heart* as well as of the mind. Edward Arlington Robinson gave a penetrating poetic insight into character through his reference to Nicodemus. He pictures Nicodemus, the distinguished member of the Sanhedrin, after his night visit to Jesus, going to the high priest Caiaphas singing the praises of this new teacher from Nazareth. But Caiaphas only smiles indulgently. He is not afraid that Nicodemus will join the company of the Nazarene. He knows his man. Hence he says to Nicodemus that he will not go from them for a mad carpenter. And Nicodemus never did go with Jesus.

The Roman centurion with his sick slave, having heard of Jesus' mighty works, believed as did Nicodemus, that this healer must possess the power of God. Very likely he also knew that the social and religious leaders looked down upon this unlettered carpenter. But the centurion was not deterred by pride from being seen with Jesus. In fact, he was so humble that he felt unworthy to ask Jesus into his house. Certainly the centurion's humble faith was a far cry from the proud posture of the worshiping Pharisees. Perhaps this was another factor which prompted Jesus to say: "Not even in Israel have I found such faith."

We note now a third feature of the centurion. He was a man of disciplined action. He said, "I am a man set under authority, with soldiers under me: and I say to one, 'Go,' and he goes; and to another, 'Come,' and he comes; and to my slave, 'Do this,' and he does it." Just as his subordinates obeyed him, he obeyed his superiors. He was a man of deeds rather than words. Chesterton once said that if he were drowning he would rather meet a burglar who could swim than a bishop who couldn't! It is action that counts.

We learn to trust by action rather than by argument. There are regions in life where action must precede conviction, where we must commit ourselves before we fully understand. Friendship is such a realm. If your friend invites you to dinner, you do not ask for a written guarantee that there is no poison in the food. If he invites you to ride with him in his car, he does not require you to sign a waiver releasing him from damages in case of accident. If your friend bids you to spend the night in his house, he does not put you under bond not to steal the valuables in the room. In short, a friend trusts himself to the fidelity of a friend.

This extension of faith, this taking of certain confidences for granted, applies in some degree to the associations of all gentlemen. Anyone who refuses to associate with others on such a basis cuts himself off from friendly intercourse.

And this attitude of trust, so essential to human fellowship, is equally necessary in our relations with God. As Charles Wishart said, we must be gentlemen with God if we are to develop faith in him.

But the centurion's trust was of a sterner and firmer quality than that which operates in ordinary friendly and gentlemanly relations. It had been developed by disciplined action. He had drilled himself in the imperatives of army commands.

Matthew Arnold, in the Preface to *Culture and Anarchy,* expressed the self-discipline essential to true faith: "To walk staunchly by the best light one has, to be strict and sincere with oneself, not to be of the number of those who say and do not, to be in earnest—this is the discipline by which alone man is enabled to rescue his life from thraldom to the passing moment and to his bodily sense, to ennoble it and to make it eternal."

The Roman centurion was living up to the best light he had. He was in deadly earnest. He was pleading for his slave's life rather than his own. He was speaking with the spirit of a soldier, a man under authority. And as a soldier who knew authority, his spirit was opened to feel the authority of Christ.

It is noteworthy that Roman officers did recognize the power and authority of Christ. Here was this centurion in Capernaum at the beginning of Christ's ministry. And there was the Roman centurion at the cross who, after watching Christ's conduct on the cross, cried: "Certainly, this man was innocent."

Now comes the centurion's statement of faith: "Say the word, and let my servant be healed." He did not ask for any argument to prove Jesus' divine power. He did not ask Jesus to go and lay his hands on his servant, for he said he was not worthy to have Jesus enter his house. He had such faith in Jesus' power that he asked him only to say the word and his slave would be healed. His quality of faith caused Jesus to marvel and exclaim: "I tell you, not even in Israel have I found such faith." Here was faith not founded in proof texts offered by scribes, not arrived at by argument, but faith grounded in trustworthy character, kept growing by humility, and developed by disciplined action.

And climaxing all this came the confidence of intuitive faith. Faith, as we have said, is not a sixth sense by which we apprehend realities for which we have no other evidence. It is our human capacity to appreciate the true significance of the reality we apprehend. It is not a substitute for our other ways of knowing; rather, it is our way of unifying what these other methods bring us.

In our most intimate and personal relationships, certainty comes to us by intuitive insight. How do I know that my friend is to be trusted or that my wife is worthy of my love? Not because I have weighed the arguments and come to a reasoned conclusion, but because there is something in me which goes out to what I find in them with an irresistible impulse. I love and trust through an intuition of faith.

Lord Balfour wrote of Alfred Lyttleton:

I will not attempt any analysis of the unique charm which makes the life of Alfred Lyttleton irreplaceable. Such an attempt would indeed be vain.

We can neither separate the whole into its parts, nor recompose the parts into the whole. There was that about him which made immediate and irresistible appeal to every man and woman whom he met, and made that appeal to what was best in them.[1]

That immediacy of appeal which Alfred Lyttleton's wholeness of personality had to Lord Balfour was akin, though in lesser degree, to the effect of the Christ upon the centurion. We human beings at some moments are carried beyond the usual range of our thinking and arrive at insights which seem to be given us from a higher wisdom. The centurion, conditioned by the trustworthiness of his character, the urgency of his desire, and the purity of his motive, was attuned to the divine response. And Christ, the God-man with his unparalleled power to inspire, granted the centurion's plea.

There was an authority revealed in Jesus' teaching which the crowds recognized because he taught "not as their scribes." There was an authority in his healing power which the learned Nicodemus perceived could not be possessed by a person unless God is with him. And here was a centurion, untutored by the scribes or the Pharisees, who realized that Jesus had an authority as real as that of a military officer, who says to his soldier, "Go," and he goes; and "Come," and he comes. Here was faith at its pure source. It evoked from Jesus the glad and grateful commendation: "I tell you, not even in Israel have I found such faith."

"And when those who had been sent returned to the house, they found the slave well."

---

[1] Edith Lyttleton, *Alfred Lyttleton, An Account of His Life* (London: 1923), Preface.

II. SINCERITY IS NOT ENOUGH

There are some persons who cross our paths only once and yet make such an impression on us that we keep looking for them a long time afterwards. One such person was Nathanael. We get our glimpse of him in the first chapter of John's Gospel. He arouses the reader's expectations. And some think that they see him again in the person of the apostle Bartholomew. Others have tried to identify him with the disciple John, and still others think that Nathanael may have been Paul. But there is not enough evidence to support these contentions. So let us look at Nathanael just as he appears in the first chapter of the Fourth Gospel.

Listen to the record:

The next day Jesus decided to go to Galilee. And he found Philip and said to him, "Follow me." Now Philip was from Bethsaida, the city of Andrew and Peter. Philip found Nathanael, and said to him, "We have found him of whom Moses in the law and also the prophets wrote, Jesus of Nazareth, the son of Joseph." Nathanael said to him, "Can anything good come out of Nazareth?"

We have read far enough to reveal one thing about Nathanael. He had a *prejudice*. Prejudice is defined as a judgment or opinion formed without the examination of the facts or reasons that are essential to a just and impartial determination. With this definition it would be true to say that our first judgments in infancy are colored by prejudice.

As a child of four or five, I was prejudiced in favor of my father. I have no record, even no recollection, of what I said at that age. But if I was normal—and I guess I was—I would not listen with an open mind and reasoned judgment when a playmate boasted that his father was stronger than mine. I had never seen his father fight mine. Yet without any visible proof, I stoutly maintained the superior strength of my paternal ancestor. In fact, on more than one occasion, I am told that I fought for my prejudice on this point.

And at other times I was prejudiced against my parents. When they refused something I desired very much, my hot little mind called them unfair. My childish judgments were not always based on reason and justice. A popular song in the play *South Pacific* carried a pertinent truth in its line, "You have to be taught to hate." The poisonous plants of racial and national dislikes are grown by cultivation, but the predisposition to prejudice is in the soil of childhood.

Nathanael had a prejudice against Nazareth as the birthplace of the Jewish Messiah. Some commentators hold that when Philip told him Jesus was from Nazareth, Nathanael's comment was tantamount to saying, "Can anything good come out of a hole like Nazareth?" Perhaps Nazareth had a bad reputation in Nathanael's social circles. Others say that his mind was closed to the possibility of the Messiah coming from a place so near and ordinary as Nazareth. It is often hard for people to believe that great historical events can take place in their own neighborhoods. When the news of the Wright brothers' history-making flight of the first power-driven airplane reached Dayton, Ohio, the story is told that some people there said, "Nobody is ever going to fly, and if anybody does fly, it won't be anybody from a place like Dayton."

Jesus faced this prejudice of provincialism. Some of his hearers did not believe in him because they knew his family. To them he was too near at hand. They said, "We know where this man comes from; and when the Christ appears, no one will know where he comes from." Other critics in Jerusalem were prejudiced against Jesus for just the opposite reason. They said: "We know that God has spoken to Moses, but as for this man, we do not know where he comes from." Prejudice is so irrational that it takes almost any form to fit the likes and dislikes of people. As Tom Paine said, prejudice is like the spider; it makes everywhere its home and thrives most where there seems nothing to feed on. The more nearly empty the mental attic, the more cobwebs of prejudice.

We all have some prejudices. Anatole France remarked of a certain person: "He flattered himself on being a man without any prejudices; and this pretension itself is a very great prejudice."

Jesus had a harder time in confronting the prejudices of the self-righteous than in converting the publicans and harlots. In the presence of Jesus' purity, the Magdalene grew repentant. In the atmosphere of Jesus' honesty, the publican, Zacchaeus, became conscientious; but the prejudiced minds of the respectable Pharisees only grew harder. After Jesus had tried vainly to soften them with the warmth of his love and to pierce them with the shafts of his arguments, he said to them bluntly, "The publicans and harlots go into the kingdom of God before you" (K.J.V.).

The sins of the mind can be so much more subtly dangerous than the sins of the body. The latter, like lust or intemperance, usually leave their open marks and thereby are likely to induce a sense of shame and a spirit of repentance. But mental sins such as prejudice and pride produce no visible physical scars which serve to check their progress. And one bigoted person in a place of power can do more damage than a dozen drunken derelicts.

Prejudice is a sin which everyone denounces and almost no one seriously confesses. Prejudiced persons do not come to the church or the confessional crying to be saved from their narrowness and bigotry. Prejudice is so difficult to dislodge because it lurks in such respectable places and so often works underground. Yet if right and reason are ever to prevail, we must confront this evil of prejudice, for it has destroyed more happiness, hindered more progress, and directly or indirectly caused more bloodshed than almost any other sin.

Let us go on with the narrative. When Nathanael voiced his prejudice against the possibility of the Messiah being found in neighboring Nazareth, Philip said, "Come and see." And Nathanael went. The second thing to be noted about him is that *he was willing to be shown.*

Philip did not argue with Nathanael. To argue with prejudice is pretty futile. Closed minds do not open to the knocks of reason, however loud and logical they may be. One reason that the pulpit ministry is currently suffering for lack of applicants is the feeling that preaching is ineffective in changing the mind-set of those in the pew. One young minister, who recently left the parish pulpit for high-school teaching, asserted his belief that he could get fewer religious ideas across to his elderly parishioners than he could to his young students, even though he was teaching secular subjects.

The fields of science appeal to youth partly because they offer concrete experiments and application. We must get more demonstration and less argument into our presentation of religion. Jesus did. The day before he met Nathanael, Jesus had been walking along the Jordan when he was observed by two disciples of John the Baptist. Jesus noted that they were following him and he asked, "What do you seek?" They said, "Teacher, where are you staying?" He replied, "Come and see." They went along. One of them was Andrew, Simon Peter's brother. Andrew hurried to tell Simon. And now Philip goes to Nathanael with the same invitation, "Come and see."

How fair and open-minded is this characteristic invitation! If you would know about Jesus Christ, come and see for yourself. Jesus was no magician or demagogue trying to cast a spell over unseeing minds. We might well say that Christ invites the scientific approach.

George Romanes, a noted British biologist and psychologist of the nineteenth century, lost his faith in God and Christ. Then it came home to him that he was not acting scientifically, for the first principle of science is that if there is evidence for a thing, we are bound to put it to the test. And since there is an abundance of evidence purporting to show that Christianity does work in changing lives, Romanes said to himself that it behooved him as an honest man of science to give this thing its chance to prove itself. He did test it. And for him it did come true.

We should be as fair with Christ as we are in our scientific pursuits. But we must remember that there is a difference between learning the facts about a chemical element in the laboratory and learning to know a living person. In a laboratory test we make our experiments, assemble the data, and then make up our minds. But in our relationship with persons we reach a point where we must make a decision and then let the future reveal more facts. In choosing a business partner or employee, we come to the point where we must make a choice on faith. In choosing a husband or wife, we do not know all about our beloved before we plight our troth. We learn by living.

The most blessed assurances of life are beyond scientific proof. There is no laboratory test that proves a mother's love, yet every mother's son is sure of it. There is no scientific way of proving the beauty of Beethoven's symphonies, yet as Browning said, "We musicians know." There is no scientific way of proving the love of God as revealed in Christ. Yet countless Christians have lived their way into that assurance, as did the apostle Paul who, after enduring persecution, famine, stoning, shipwreck, could confidently declare, "I know whom I have believed and I am sure that he is able to guard until that Day what has been entrusted to me."

Nathanael had a prejudice against the idea of the Messiah coming out of Nazareth, but he was willing to go and see. Now let us get on with the story. Jesus saw Nathanael coming and said, "Behold, an Israelite indeed, in whom is no guile!" The third feature, therefore, we note in Nathanael is that he was *sincere*.

Jesus welcomed Nathanael with a tribute to his sincerity. He might have referred to the man's provincialism and prejudice. But he warmed the cold and skeptical mind of Nathanael by saying, "An Israelite . . . , in whom is no guile." This greeting was characteristic of Jesus. Recall how he called the dishonest publican Zacchaeus a "son of Abraham."

Ordinarily, the surest way to get the best out of a person is to say the best thing you can say of him. Call a man a thief and he is likely to conclude that he might as well have the game with the name. Tell your child he is a fool and he will very probably justify the appellation. We are to challenge people to live up to the names we give them. We are to give names to live up to, not down to. Never is a sinner so ashamed of his fault as when he knows that something better is expected of him.

Nathanael's heart and mind picked up when Jesus called him "an Israelite . . . , in whom is no guile." About the most genuine compliment a person can receive is to be called sincere. Sincerity is to character what the spinal cord is to the human body. Motion, sensation, nerve energy—all are dependent on its healthy existence. Opinions, to be worth anything, must be sincerely held.

Abbé Dimnet, of France, whose book *The Art of Thinking* had such wide acceptance after the last war, said that we must be ourselves if we are to create anything original. And he added that the chief obstacles to a person's being himself are pretense and diffidence. When a person uses up his energy in pretending to be what he is not, how can he give himself to the business of being himself?

Jesus condemned the hypocrisy of the Pharisees because it kept them from being true to themselves, their fellow men, or their God. And for the same fundamental reasons Christ condemns the current forms of hypocrisy. His counsel comes as clearly to us as to his first disciples: "Beware of the leaven of the Pharisees, which is hypocrisy."

The complexity of living adds to the strain of pretense. We try to keep up on so many fronts. We should seek the simple essentials within the superimposed complexities. Jesus said, "If . . . thine eye be single, thy whole body shall be full of light." (K.J.V.) With an eye single to truth and to God, we can lessen the strain of pretense and the strut of hypocrisy by cutting loose from the cult of comparisons.

When a person is on guard to hide his real self from the gaze of those whose good opinion he seeks; when he is struggling to maintain a reputation better than his true character; when he is putting up a bold front to conceal inner weakness and emptiness—that is a strain. It shows in furtive glances, in a nervous hurry to put over a good impression before there is time for sober and searching second thoughts. The strain shows in a general feeling of insecurity.

Jesus made so much of genuineness. He worked from within out. "Cleanse the inside of the cup." Guard the eye from the lustful look. Keep anger out of the heart, for "out of it are the issues of life" (K.J.V.). He counseled his followers that they must be sound at the core.

Some years ago Anne Morrow Lindbergh wrote an article on "The Most Unforgettable Character I Ever Met." The person was Edward Sheldon, the playwright. He had a play on Broadway before he had finished his graduate work at Harvard. Several successes followed. His career gave promise of exceptional brilliance. But in his late twenties he was stricken with a cruel and progressive form of arthritis, which left him a rigid body without vision or motion and with only his ears and his voice. Yet so triumphantly genuine was his character and so piercing his powers of perception that, said Mrs. Lindbergh, when you entered his room, he instantly seemed to know all about you outwardly and inwardly. He saw you whole, and in his presence you felt whole. She said: "The beautiful prayer from the Phaedrus was answered, 'The outward and the inward man were at one.'"

When our external attitudes tally with our inner spirit, we are no longer under strain of pretense. Then we can apply our whole individual selves to the task at hand. Then we have strength and creative power. As Sir Galahad said,

> My strength is as the strength of ten,
> Because my heart is pure.

A new birth of sincerity is essential to worthy coexistence in families, in communities, and in the international realm. Our social circles are poisoned by polite insincerities. We cannot always be sure that our friends tell us the truth, the whole truth, and nothing but the truth. They wish to be tactful. They so often tell us the thing which they think we would like to hear. And, alas, if they don't, they so often cease to be our friends!

Sincerity in speech is essential to all healthy fellowship. When Jesus warned against taking the name of the Lord in vain, we assume that he was inveighing against what we call profanity. He was. But he was attacking something deeper; namely, the profaning of speech by insincerity. Hence he said, "Let what you say be simply 'Yes' or 'No'; anything more than this comes from evil." We often avoid candor in speech in order to be pleasing. We think that insincere tact "heals many wounds." We should remember Dorothy Parker's tart comment that we need honest speech which "wounds many heels." Sincerity in speech includes fairness and honesty in controversy, scorning to take an unfair advantage in argument, or trying to make the worse appear the better reason.

In the realm of business to find a man without guile is heartening. Every article of valuable manufacture is imitated in a cheaper form. Man's inventive genius can be employed to improve the quality and usefulness of products, but it can also be used to produce cheaper substitutes which look as good or better than the original, but lack its lasting values. The men without guile who refuse to adulterate their products and advertise them falsely are the pillars of business and industry.

A certain man of my acquaintance by his training and ability gave promise of becoming a leader in his line of work. He was pleasing in his appearance and always plausible in his statements. But he was not sincerely loyal to those above him. He was not honest in admitting his mistakes, always trying to shift the blame to others, friendly to their faces and critical behind their backs. The result was that he failed to rise to first place, but got shunted off into second-rate responsibilities. He isolated himself from the channels of promotion by his insincerity. Leadership goes to the persons of sincere loyalties.

In religion, sincerity is essential to the acquisition of sound, strong faith. There must be a real and genuine desire to know and follow the will of God, although it may oppose our own individual prejudices and run counter to the popular approval. A sincere state of the heart is as necessary to the reception of religious truth as is an enlightened state of the understanding.

This is the point in the beatitude, "Blessed are the pure in heart, for they shall see God." James Moffatt once said in class that the beatitude should be translated thus: "Blessed are they who are not double-minded, for they shall be admitted into the intimate presence of God." The double-minded person is not without guile. He thinks one way and speaks another. He has at least two reasons for what he does—a good reason which he announces and the real reason which he keeps to himself. If we wish to make sure of God, we must first try to make ourselves the kind of persons of whom God and our fellow men can be sure. The pure in heart are not double-minded, deceiving themselves and others. They are without guile, single-minded and wholehearted.

Nathanael was sincere, without guile in his mind and with purity of motive in his heart. He was therefore prepared to approach Christ. We continue the record. When Jesus greeted Nathanael with the words, "An Israelite indeed, in whom is no guile," Nathanael said, "How do you know me?" Jesus answered him, "Before Philip called you, when you were under the fig tree, I saw you." That expression is suggestive of several rabbinical references to a seat under the fig tree as the right place for the study of the Torah. Jesus is thus praising Nathanael as a true searcher of the Scriptures. Nathanael did not blushingly deprecate himself by denying the tributes of Jesus. He showed his frank, straightforward attitude by accepting them. And he was swept out of his prejudice and skepticism by a surge of conviction. He cried, "Rabbi, you are the Son of God! You are the King of Israel!" Jesus answered him, "Because I said to you, I saw you under the fig tree, do you believe? You shall see greater things than these."

Nathanael's prejudice against a Messiah from Nazareth has now given way to an open, frank, sincere acceptance. The impulsive confession of his conviction is a tribute to the immediate impression which Jesus made. Jesus had something about his personality, his power of mind, his magnetic force, which impressed those who came to him with open, sincere minds. Sincerity is the essential state of mind in which to approach Christ.

Nevertheless, sincerity is not enough. It is only the starting point of discipleship. Christ had greater things to show Nathanael. He made this same point with other Israelites later in his ministry. In the eighth chapter of John we are told of certain Jews who believed in Jesus because of what they heard him say and saw him do. But Jesus said, "If you continue in my word, you are truly my disciples, and you will know the truth, and the truth will make you free."

The members of that audience apparently did not go on to become disciples of Christ. And we cannot be absolutely sure about Nathanael because he is not mentioned by that name elsewhere, except in a passage which is considered to be a later addition to John's gospel. And how about ourselves? We may be so impressed by a few glimpses of Christ that, like Nathanael, we exclaim, "You are the Son of God! You are the King of Israel!" But we never press on into the fullness of truth that was in Christ. We never grow up in the grace and knowledge of Christ.

If we are to be disciples of Christ we must continue in his word until we advance from sincerity to truth. We are sincere when our words and behavior tally with our beliefs. We are disciples of Christ only when our words and actions and beliefs tally with the truth. The Spanish Inquisitors in the sixteenth century were many of them sincere when they burned at the stake those whom they called heretics because they did not conform to the beliefs of the church. The Puritans of Massachusetts Bay, when they drove out Roger Williams, no doubt sincerely believed that they were right and he was wrong.

"The heart," said the prophet Jeremiah, "is deceitful above all things." Our desires and feelings may deceive us into believing something with all our hearts and yet that something may not be true or right. At the close of the Revolutionary War in 1783, Washington, Jefferson, and a great many other Southerners were willing to end Negro slavery. But the New England traders, who were making good profit in the African slave traffic, were for perpetuating the system. In 1860, when the cotton gin had made cotton profitable with slave labor, the South defended slavery, while the North declared it was of the devil. In both sections self-interest colored their convictions but the reversal of sides illustrates how views may be distorted by angles of vision and self-interest.

Various are the ways by which we may be sincere and yet fail to be true. If I am to be true to myself I must be true to my real self. And I am not always my real self. When I am depressed or churlish or angry, I am not my real self. Haven't we often heard the expression, "He wasn't himself this morning." So often we quote Shakespeare's words:

> This above all: To thine own self be true,
> And it must follow, as the night the day,
> Thou canst not then be false to any man."

We are prone to think that is the complete formula for honest, straightforward living. But it is not. Suppose that those words had been spoken to Hamlet rather than to Laertes: would the distraught Hamlet have known what being true to himself implied? Christ comes both to bid us to be true to ourselves and also to show us what our true selves really are.

In *The Bridge of San Luis Rey* Thornton Wilder told the story of Uncle Pio, the singing master, who took a talented but rather vain and superficial girl from a South American music hall and tried to develop her into a genuine artist. She became a popular singer, but she fed her pride on the crowd's applause and was content with a mediocre performance, if the public seemed to approve. But each night, when she turned from the footlights to leave the stage, she found her old master standing in the wings. He was not fooled by the applause. He knew the possibilities of her talent and he dedicated himself to developing her true self.

So with us on the stage of life. The crowd may applaud or condemn. But One there is who stands within the wings. It is Christ the Master

31

we must face, and with him we must be simple, sincere, and real.

Jesus' last words to Nathanael were, "Truly, truly, I say to you, you will see heaven opened, and the angels of God ascending and descending upon the Son of man." This figure of speech was an allusion to the experience of Jacob, an Israelite in whom there was guile. After Jacob had cheated his brother Esau out of his birthright, he fled from his father's country. Out in the wilderness, the homesick young man had a dream one night in which he saw the heavens opened and a ladder reaching up to heaven and the Lord standing above it saying, "I am the Lord, the God of Abraham your father and the God of Isaac." And when Jacob awoke, he said, "Surely the Lord is in this place; and I did not know it."

Jacob, the dishonest cheater of his brother, his father, and his father-in-law, was transformed into the spiritual head of his people. How? Not merely by being cured of his guile but by continuing to grow in mind and heart.

When we are led by the light of God, we see things which are invisible to the natural eye. I have walked through gardens with members of garden clubs. They have seen subtle distinctions and niceties of cultivation which missed my eye. I have visited art museums with artists, and their knowledge put my limited appreciation to shame. I have visited cathedrals with spiritually minded companions whose mystical insights have left me comparatively unmoved.

Moreover, when the Lord sends out his light to lead us, he helps us to consider the factors which the natural eye cannot measure. There are certain imponderable elements in every situation. For example, we can compute the tensile strength of a bar of iron, but we cannot compute so exactly the lifting power of the person who uses the bar, for, under certain conditions, the same person may lift two, three, or four times as much as he can under other conditions. We can measure the horsepower of engines but not the man power of engineers. The human equation cannot be computed in statistical charts.

When Hitler marched into Paris, pictures were taken showing the

Führer dancing in glee. But the *New York Times* had an editorial containing these words:

> It is only the lovely shell that Hitler has captured. He has not captured the true Paris. Never can he, his tanks, his robot battalions penetrate within the walls of that magic city. . . . Paris where democracy had its modern rebirth; Paris that taught the world to paint and build . . . Paris of museums, libraries, universities in which the mind could range at will; Paris the spiritual, Paris the city of love, Paris the city of light . . . this is not Hitler's Paris, not today, not ever.

And so it proved. You cannot "nazify" a nation's culture with a *blitzkrieg*. There are immeasurable forces and values back of the Louvre, back of the Sorbonne, back of Notre Dame, which the Nazis could not destroy and which the communists cannot compute.

Ah, what vast vistas of revelation are given to those who continue to study the truth as it was in God and Christ! What holy places where the Lord is and we do not know it! What unsearchable riches there are in Christ! What new dimensions are to be discovered in "the breadth and length and depth and height of that love which surpasses knowledge" and which we saw on the cross.

Nathanael was sincere, an Israelite in whom was no guile. Sincerity is the proper state in which to start with Christ. But the Christian must go on to make his sincerity safe for truth, safe for the church, safe for the world. Sincerity may be misguided into error and slavery and war. Only those who "grow in the grace and knowledge of our Lord Jesus Christ" are really his disciples.

To stop growing is a sin. A mind may be stunted through being uninformed. If I let my mind remain in ignorance, that is a sin. Others may not be sufficiently conscious of my mental emptiness to condemn me for it. I may not even know what I am missing. But even in the eyes of statute law, ignorance does not quite excuse me, does it? If I run my business in a way that violates the tax regulations, I am not exonerated by pleading that I did not know the law. If I unintentionally kill my friend with a gun which I did not know was loaded, I may not be charged with murder, but I cannot forgive myself.

And in the eyes of Christ ignorance does not excuse me. Recall Jesus' description of the Last Judgment. He said:

"I was hungry and you gave me no food, I was thirsty and you gave me no drink, I was a stranger and you did not welcome me, naked and you did not clothe me, sick and in prison and you did not visit me." Then they also will answer: "Lord, when did we see thee hungry or thirsty or a stranger or naked or sick or in prison, and did not minister to thee?" Then he will answer them, "Truly, I say to you, as you did it not to one of the least of these, you did it not to me."

Theirs was the sin of not noticing and not knowing.

Jesus came to set our minds on the trail of truth. He came to make us alive to the world around us—its people, its beauty, its needs. And not to be alive to what we should be aware of is a form of sin. Others may not denounce us. But we cannot get away with it in the eyes of Christ.

Nathanael was worthy of praise for his sincerity. He had his prejudices, but with the help of Philip and Jesus he opened his mind and heart to God. His plain, blunt, straightforward nature raised our hopes of great things. But where was Nathanael later when Jesus was doing the "greater things" which he promised to show him? Where was Nathanael the night of the Last Supper and the day of the Crucifixion? Nathanael apparently failed to go on seeing with Jesus and he dropped out of sight.

Do you know of any church named after "Saint Nathanael"?

III. WHERE LAW MEETS LOVE

The residents of New York City are familiar with a stretch of water known as Hell Gate. It is the place where the current of the Harlem River meets waters and tides of Long Island Sound. Its ominous name, Hell Gate, is due to the roughness of the water.

Wherever currents meet in diverse directions it is rough, whether it be in the water, the air, or the life of man. When the war was on between the North and the South, it was in border cities like Baltimore and in border states like Kentucky, Kansas, and Missouri that tensions were sharpest. There loyalties were divided in the same communities, even in the same families.

And crosscurrents cause conflict within an individual life. A person may be torn between duty and desire, between love and honor, between the pull of the past and the push of the future.

Yet in all the history of the Christian faith, there is no figure in whom the conflicting currents met more roughly than in John the Baptist. He stood on the border between the law of the old covenant and the love of the new. A fiery evangelist, preaching reform and righteousness, he was lifted to the height of popularity by the crowds flocking to hear him. From this pinnacle he was dragged down to prison by King Herod, whose sins he had condemned. While he was imprisoned, John was troubled by doubts of his own work. He had heralded the coming of the Messiah and had baptized a young Jesus of Nazareth who, as he thought, would usher in the expected kingdom of God. But the reports of Jesus' work did not fit John's pattern. Hence, from his prison John sent messengers to Jesus, asking: "Are you he who is to come, or shall we look for another?"

Jesus sent back word to tell John what they had seen and heard, how the lepers were cleansed, the blind received their sight, and to the poor the gospel was preached. Then after the deputation had departed, Jesus turned to the crowd and began to talk about John. He asked the crowd, "What did you go out into the wilderness to behold? A reed shaken by the wind?" No. John was no weak reed, no pliable seeker of popularity bending with every gust of public opinion. Jesus asked again, "What then did you go out to see? A man clothed in soft raiment? Behold, those who are gorgeously appareled and live in luxury are in kings' courts." John was no caterer to kings, no private chaplain to the rich and powerful.

Jesus went on. "What then did you go out to see? A prophet? Yes, I tell you, and more than a prophet." And Jesus climaxed his tribute to John with these words, "I tell you, among those born of women none is greater than John."

Then Jesus added this arresting statement, "Yet he who is least in the kingdom of God is greater than he."

How are we to understand these puzzling words, as they are recorded in the seventh chapter of Luke and also in the eleventh chapter of Matthew? John the Baptist, heroically brave, incorruptibly honest, self-sacrificing to the point of giving his own life, standing at the threshold of the Kingdom and yet not in it! What did John lack that Christ came to give?

Pause a moment longer to consider the high praise Jesus gave to John. John, he said, was no weak reed swaying with the winds of popular opinion. He was not a weathervane; he was a guidepost.

John's sturdy independence was derived from God and disciplined in solitude. Before his preaching crusade along the Jordan, the Baptist had immersed himself in the wilderness.

Nansen, the explorer, has reminded us that the great reformers who have left their mark in history came out of seclusion. Recall the case of Moses, who found his mission in the solitude of the wilderness. Amos, the roughly clothed vinedresser working alone with God in his vineyard, caught his prophetic message which aroused Israel's conscience. Saul of Tarsus, after his experience on the Damascus road, went away for a long period into the seclusion of the Arabian desert. Go beyond the bounds of the Bible and think of Gautama Buddha, rapt in meditation under the bo tree. John in his preaching along the Jordan drew great crowds, but he did not seek them by saying what was popular.

But he was "more than a prophet." In fulfilling his mission John was more than a spokesman for God. He was a forerunner of God's new era of redemption. He was preparing the way for One greater than himself, "the latchet of whose shoes I am not worthy to unloose." (K.J.V.) He humbly recognized his own subordination to the sovereignty of the Coming One and declared it. "He must increase, but I must decrease."

Yet with all John's integrity, his courage, his devotion, Jesus asserted: "He who is least in the kingdom of God is greater than he."

Some feel that John was thus put by Jesus outside the pale of salvation. They reason that all who died before accepting Jesus as the Christ were doomed to eternal hell. They cite Jesus' words: "No man cometh unto the Father, but by me." (K.J.V.) They would thus exclude John the Baptist, and all Jews and others who died before Christ's time. To avoid such a conclusion, some insert in the Apostles' Creed the words: "He descended into hell." This statement is based on the words of I Pet. 3:19: "He went and preached to the spirits in prison." The idea here is that Christ, between his crucifixion and resurrection, descended into hell in order to preach the gospel to those who had died before his time and thus give them the chance of salvation.

Other churches omit the words, "He descended into hell," from their version of the Apostles' Creed partly because they believe that God as a Father judges people according to their light and makes allowance for those who lived in pre-Christian times, and also because they believe in the pre-existent Christ as John's Gospel presents him in the Prologue: "In the beginning was the Word, and the Word was with God, and the Word was God," before the "Word became flesh and dwelt among us." Jesus said, "Before Abraham was, I am." The eternal Christ existed from the beginning. Hence, he did not need to descend into hell after the crucifixion to give men a chance of salvation.

We do not hold that John the Baptist was excluded from salvation because Jesus said: "He who is least in the kingdom of God is greater than [John]." It is, of course, presumptuous for us to define what was in Jesus' mind. But in the light of the context and Jesus' later conduct, commentators conclude that Jesus, with all his respect and love for John, was pointing out John's failure to grasp the secret of the kingdom of heaven.

For one thing, John did not comprehend the *nature* of the kingdom of God as Jesus proclaimed it. John's message might be summed up, "Repent, for the day of judgment is coming." He denounced the wrongs to be righted. He expected a Messiah to come in some dramatic way to overthrow the existing political regime and rearrange the social system.

But this Jesus of Nazareth, whom he had baptized as the expected Messiah, was working so contrary to John's expectation. He led no revolt to overturn the existing order and free his people from the Roman yoke. He went about teaching and healing, working quietly without any great publicized dramatic demonstrations.

Jesus was ever talking about the kingdom of God, or kingdom of heaven. He used many parables to describe it. Yet when the Pharisees asked when the kingdom of God was coming, he answered: "The kingdom of God is not coming with signs to be observed; nor will they say, 'Lo, here it is!' or 'There!' for behold, the kingdom of God is in the midst of you."

If we would try to comprehend Christ's concept of the Kingdom, we must go back to the beginning of the Gospels. Mark asserts that the first public utterance of Jesus after his baptism and temptation in the wilderness was: "The time is fulfilled, and the kingdom of God is at hand." In the Gospel of Matthew the expression occurs some fifty times. Jesus was on fire with it. But he found it hard to describe. He tried to express it in one image, or parable, after another. He insisted that it is the greatest thing in life. It is like a treasure hidden in a field; that is to say, it is not something that men see as a matter of course and by nature. Nor is it something that can be found all at once and kept like a treasure. It grows in men's minds like a seed. Its beginning is small, like a grain of mustard seed, but when it is grown, it is the greatest of all herbs. It is both outside us and within us.

"The kingdom . . . is at hand." It exists wherever God's will rules. We would make it clearer to ourselves if we spoke of the "kingship of God" rather than the "kingdom of God." When we think of kingdoms we think of geographical areas, like the kingdom of Belgium or the kingdom of Sweden. There is no land area on this planet whose inhabitants submit wholly to the rule of God. But there are areas of life in which God rules. Hence, we can say the kingship of God is at hand—in fact, has always been here.

God the creator of heaven and earth is the ruler of his physical creation. He holds the stars in their courses and gives the harvests in their season.

The Russians have tauntingly boasted that their space explorations have exploded the biblical theories of God. Their argonauts have found no God or angels in the heavens. True, the modern sputniks have disproved the naïve teaching of the czaristic church which peopled the heavens with winged spirits, but the scientific calculations and achievements of the spacemen have demonstrated the orderliness of this created universe. The recent Telstar "declares the glory of God" and the orbiting of the globe "showeth his handiwork." The kingdom of God is at hand in the heavens even though we searchers for the moon may be far from it in our motives of competition. The rule of God is at hand as the light is round about us, but only as we open our eyes do we rejoice in the light.

The kingship of God is at hand as the truth is round about our minds, but only those minds which are seeking the truth find it. That was the point Jesus tried to make before Pilate when Pilate asked him, "Are you the King of the Jews?" . . . Jesus answered: "My kingship is not of this world; if my kingship were of this world, my servants would fight, that I might not be handed over to the Jews; but my kingship is not from this world." Pilate said, "So you are a king?" Jesus answered, "You say that I am a king. For this was I born, and for this I have come into the world, to bear witness to the truth. Every one who is of the truth hears my voice."

The kingdom of heaven was at hand in Pilate's court. It was not a matter of space but of spirit. Jesus was in the Kingdom at that moment; Pilate was not, although he was in the same room. The person sitting beside you in church may be in the kingdom of heaven because he has entered into the mind and spirit of Christ and has allowed the will of God to rule his heart. The person on the other side may be not far from the kingdom of God—as was the lawyer who answered Jesus so correctly about the first and great commandment.

Yes, the kingdom of heaven is already in our midst even in a world as sinful as ours. This nature of the Kingdom as Jesus portrayed it was not comprehended by John the Baptist. He was looking for a visible dramatic political establishment of divine rule.

Nor did John understand Jesus' *methods* of entering the kingdom of heaven. Jesus gave us several suggestions. One was by way of the childlike spirit. The disciples once asked Jesus "Who is the greatest in the kingdom of heaven?" And calling to him a child, he put the little one in the midst and said, "Truly, I say to you, unless you turn and become like children, you will never enter the kingdom of heaven. Whoever humbles himself like this child, he is the greatest in the kingdom of heaven."

And again when parents were bringing little children to him to bless them, he said, "Let the children come to me, do not hinder them; for to such belongs the kingdom of God. Truly, I say to you, whoever does not receive the kingdom of God like a child shall not enter it."

It is the childlike spirit, open-minded, free from prejudices, and sensitive to things spiritual—such is one channel by which we come into the Kingdom.

Another condition of entrance is "to have eyes to see" and "ears to hear." Thornton Wilder, in his play *Our Town,* reminds us poignantly how insensitive we are to the color and flavor and beauty of our everyday life. The girl cried, "Look at me, Mother. You never had time on earth." Carl Sandburg in "Nocturne in a Deserted Brickyard" sees the moonlight "a wide dreaming pansy of an old pond in the night." Joyce Kilmer sees a tree with "a nest of robins in her hair." And Wordsworth finds in the meanest flower thoughts "that lie too deep for tears."

Still another way of entrance Jesus suggested in his beatitude, "Blessed are the poor in spirit, for theirs is the kingdom of heaven." Who are the "poor in spirit"? They are those who do not insist on their rights, who do not make demands on what they want. They do not ask what use they can derive from a thing, but they try to appreciate it for what it is in itself. The poor in spirit are those who paradoxically get the goodness of a thing because they do not think about what good they are going to get out of it.

This paradoxical principle may be observed, for instance, in relation to music. If a person goes to hear an opera in order to be able to discuss it at a forthcoming dinner party, or to broaden his general culture, or to be seen by his fellow boxholders, or to relax his nerves in the interest of his health—if he is trying to get the good of the opera for any such self-interested ends, he will never enter fully into the beauty and enjoyment of the music. If one is to enter really into the enjoyment of the composer's work, he must forget himself and his demands and allow himself to fall in love with the music. Beauty is a kingdom to which one must become selflessly subject. Only as he surrenders to the spell can he enter fully into the enjoyment.

This requirement for admission holds good when we turn from

the realm of art to the sphere of truth. The hardheaded, practical fellows sneered at Galileo as they saw him dropping objects from Pisa's leaning tower in his effort to test the relationship between weight and speed. No doubt they said, "What good will it do him when he discovers it?" Yet as it turned out, many of the inventions and discoveries of greatest use originated in experiments motivated by no practical purpose. No truths have been more useful in the long human struggle than the abstract truths which we call mathematical. Yet they were discovered and evolved by men who saw no use in them, and they would not have been found at all if the aim had been to make use of them. Truth is a kingdom which belongs to those who give themselves to it, lead where it may, cost what it will, use or no use.

The old adage, "Necessity is the mother of invention," needs a footnote. It is true only if we include in the feeling of necessity the need to satisfy man's innate hunger for truth. Just as men will risk their lives to climb mountain peaks which cannot be cultivated, so men will pursue truth for the sheer love of learning it.

This law of entrance applies to love, as well as to art and science. In real love the lover is swept off his feet; he is lifted out of himself. Love is something he surrenders to, something he forgets himself in. Love is a kingdom which belongs to the poor in spirit who are not asking for their own rights or looking for their own profit, but who give themselves gratefully in self-surrender.

Even the most earthbound persons have had some glimpses into one or more of these kingdoms. Some have been lifted out of themselves by listening to great symphonies or by looking at masterpieces of painting. Some have experienced the thrill of the scholar in the pursuit of truth, when physical hunger was forgotten and the joy of the search banished all thought of its profit. Some have known the ecstasy of falling in love.

And the kingdom of heaven is the union of these ultimate goals and values—beauty, truth, love, goodness. E. F. Scott sums it up thus: "By the Kingdom he meant the new age foretold in apocalyptic, but it was identified in his mind with a higher order of things over against the present earthly one. He thought of this order as accessible to men in their inward life, and as manifesting itself in right action and in the right relation of men to one another." [1]

When Jesus talked so much about the kingdom of heaven, was he not trying to tell his hearers that these realms into which we get occasional fleeting glimpses can become our zones of living if we surrender ourselves to their spell? Can we not test for ourselves the expansive enrichment of life which comes when we cease looking for the use and profit of things and give ourselves to the enjoyment of friends, the deep satisfactions of family blessings, the companionship of little children, the dewy freshness of new days, the glory of autumnal forests, the ageless creations of art, the contemplation of the goodness of God who made them all?

John did not understand Jesus' methods of realizing the kingdom; hence, his *ways of working were different.*

For one thing, both John and Jesus went into the wilderness where they disciplined their spirits in solitude, but with differing motives and results.

John's attitude was somewhat like that of Henry David Thoreau in our American tradition. After graduation from Harvard, Thoreau turned aside from the occupations and professions other young men were choosing and went to live in the woods. He had no ambition to make money or a name. He lived what we would call a hand-to-mouth existence, but it was really a hand-to-mind existence. He tells us why he withdrew from the world:

I went to the woods because I wished to live deliberately, to front only the essential facts of life, and see if I could not learn what it had to teach, and not, when I came to die, discover that I had not lived. . . . I wanted

[1] *Man and Society in the New Testament* (New York: Charles Scribner's Sons, 1946), p. 62.

to live deep and suck out all the marrow of life, to live so sturdily and Spartan-like as to put to rout all that was not life.[2]

By such austere living and seclusion, Thoreau achieved an integrity of character and a penetrating insight which led admirers to put him in the highest niche of greatness. He was recently installed in the Hall of Fame for Great Americans—our nation's highest accolade of greatness. Yet listen to Emerson, his admirer, as he writes: "No equal companion stood in affectionate relations with one so pure and guileless. 'I love Henry,' said one of his friends, 'but I cannot like him; and as for taking his arm, I should as soon think of taking the arm of an elm tree!'" [3]

Now, in contrast to Emerson's reference to Thoreau, listen to what Gertrude Lawrence's husband, Richard Aldrich, said of the great and greatly loved actress: "Gertrude, more than anyone I knew, dedicated her solitariness to love. All her work for, and her generous gifts to, others were illumined by love. She wanted to help people, severally and en masse, because she loved people." [4]

If that be true, then Gertrude Lawrence, more than Thoreau, caught the secret of Christ's aloneness in the wilderness. Jesus went alone not just to live "sturdily and Spartanlike," but to prepare for his redemptive mission of love. And with that purpose, Jesus found a sustaining and softening help in his solitude. Mark says, "The angels ministered to him." It was the scriptural way of describing the response which Jesus felt in his aloneness. He was alone but not lonely. Thus solitude for him became a school of love.

John emerged from the wilderness to stress the judgment of God.

He said therefore to the multitudes that came out to be baptized by him, "You brood of vipers! Who warned you to flee from the wrath to come? Bear fruits that befit repentance, and do not begin to say to yourselves, 'We

---

[2] "Where I Lived, and What I Lived For," from *Walden.*

[3] "Essay on Thoreau."

[4] From *Gertrude Lawrence as Mrs. A.* Used by permission of Pickering Press and Richard Stoddard Aldrich.

have Abraham as our father'; for I tell you, God is able from these stones to raise up children to Abraham. Even now the ax is laid to the root of the trees; every tree therefore that does not bear good fruit is cut down and thrown into the fire."

Contrast John's message with that of Jesus when he came forth from his temptation experience in the wilderness. He returned to his home town of Nazareth. As was his custom he went to the synagogue on the sabbath day. He was asked to read. He opened the Scripture and read from Isaiah:

> The Spirit of the Lord is upon me,
> because he has anointed me to preach good news to the poor.
> He has sent me to proclaim release to the captives
> and recovering of sight to the blind,
> to set at liberty those who are oppressed,
> to proclaim the acceptable year of the Lord.

John lived aloof from the society that was going to be destroyed. Jesus mingled with people. The world wasn't bad in Jesus' eyes. It is worth living in. "I came that [you] may have life, and have it abundantly." But in the midst of all our seeking, Jesus bade us remember this: "Seek first the kingdom of God, and his righteousness" (K.J.V.) and then these other things fall into their proper secondary place. John talked down to people. Jesus picked up little children. Jesus was a shepherd taking his lambs in his arms. John had his eye on the law to keep the law. Jesus was keeping the love. Jesus was a creator. John said the ax is laid at the foot of the tree, and the fruitless tree is being cast into the fire. When Jesus came, he did not use the figure of laying the ax at the root of the tree. He did liken himself once to a gardener, pleading for more time to dig around a barren tree to make it grow.

Jesus came with a spade as well as an ax. He cleared the ground, but by methods designed to make it a garden. The propagandist or social reformer has his eye on the ills to be removed; the worker with Christ considers the means of their removal, for he knows that the means shape the ends. The reformer is primarily concerned to preserve the moral order; the citizen of the Kingdom aims at the redemption of the wrongdoer.

At this point is to be found the distinction between righteousness and goodness. The apostle Paul knew this difference. Fired with righteous indignation, young Saul of Tarsus set out to rid Israel of what he considered the subversive sect of the Christus. Later, when his righteousness had been converted and mellowed into goodness, he wrote immortally of the love that "suffereth long, and is kind" (K.J.V.).

His own transforming experience throws revealing light on his statement: "Scarcely for a righteous man will one die: yet peradventure for a good man some would even dare to die." (K.J.V.) A grim reformer will die for his cause, but not many will die for a dour reformer. On the other hand, genuine goodness kindles affection. Righteousness may generate passion, but goodness has the power of compassion. The former may destroy vices; the latter makes virtues to grow in their place.

John the Baptist came as a heroic prophet and reformer proclaiming the day of judgment to be at hand. He bravely died for his principles and program. For all this Jesus commended him, saying, "Among those born of woman none is greater than John."

Jesus came with his cross not "to condemn the world; but that the world through him might be saved" (K.J.V.). He manifested such love that multitudes have been willing to die for him. This was a secret of the kingdom of heaven which John the Baptist did not comprehend. Hence Jesus could say, "He who is least in the kingdom . . . is greater than [John]."

IV. CLOSE TO THE KINGDOM

Familiar is the old saying, "A miss is as good as a mile." The import of that statement depends on the circumstances. If, for instance, we are approaching a railroad crossing as a train bears down upon us and we succeed in stopping our car within six feet of the track, we are as safe as if we had halted a mile back. In that case a miss is as good as a mile.

But suppose that we are intending to take a train and arrive just a second after the gate closes. And suppose the catching of that train would have meant success in a very important crisis, then the very narrowness of the margin by which we missed it would have added to our disappointment. Is it not true that sometimes a miss is worse than a mile, that our closeness to a successful issue only serves to deepen the sadness of missing it? One thinks of a ship's captain who has sailed the seas without a blot on his record, and then on his last voyage before retirement runs his vessel aground.

Yes, there is tragedy in missing by a margin. As Browning put it in "Saul":

> The little more, and how much it is,
> The little less, and what worlds away!

And when we think of our spiritual welfare, this margin of missing becomes of deep, even eternal, significance. What about the man to Whom Jesus said, "You are not far from the kingdom of God"? There

47

is no record that he ever crossed the border into God's kingdom. So near and yet he missed.

The Hebrew lawyer Jesus thus commended had heard him discussing with the Sadducees the hypothetical question of the woman who had been married in turn to seven brothers. The Sadducee hecklers thought they could discomfit the Nazarene carpenter by asking whose wife she would be in the resurrection realm. Jesus' answer was so skillful that it stirred the admiration of the lawyer.

And seeing that he answered them well, [the scribe] asked him, "Which commandment is the first of all?" Jesus answered, "The first is, 'Hear, O Israel: The Lord our God, the Lord is one; and you shall love the Lord your God with all your heart, and with all your soul, and with all your mind, and with all your strength.' The second is this, 'You shall love your neighbor as yourself.' There is no other commandment greater than these." And the scribe said to him, "You are right, Teacher; you have truly said that he is one, and there is no other but he; and to love him with all the heart, and with all the understanding, and with all the strength, and to love one's neighbor as oneself, is much more than all whole burnt offerings and sacrifices."

After hearing this intelligent and discreet answer of the scribe, Jesus gave him this praise: "You are not far from the kingdom of God."

The lawyer had come close to the Kingdom. What did he still lack? Mark's Gospel carries the conversation no further. For light we must look to some other statements of Jesus which present the requirements of entrance to the Kingdom.

One of these is found in the eighth chapter of John and was spoken in a situation somewhat parallel to this of the lawyer. Jesus had been discussing various aspects of his work and relationship to God. The record is, "As he spoke thus, many believed in him." But it goes on: "Jesus then said to the Jews who had believed in him, 'If you continue in my word, you are truly my disciples, and you will know the truth, and the truth will make you free.'"

There were many in Israel besides the lawyer now under consideration who accepted some of Jesus' teachings. In his early ministry the common people heard him gladly for he seemed to speak "as one having authority." Even the learned Nicodemus was impressed and attracted. The crowds were pleased and comforted when Jesus said: "Do not be anxious about your life, what you shall eat or what you shall drink. . . . Look at the birds of the air: . . . your heavenly Father feeds them. Are you not of more value than they?" The people of that day as in ours craved peace of mind and they liked it when Jesus lessened their anxiety and tensions.

And how the devout must have been delighted when Jesus said, "Ask, and it will be given you; seek and you will find." Prayer is a popular subject when people think they can use it to secure their desires.

There were those who gladly sought company with Jesus when he was such a delightful comrade as on the day of the wedding in Cana. But when he turned to denounce the social iniquities and personal impurities, the "good fellows" deserted Jesus.

There were probably many businessmen in Israel who seconded the sound honesty and practical wisdom stressed by Jesus. No doubt they said, as do many in our day, "That is good common sense. Such pleas for personal industry and integrity are good for business." But then they heard Jesus saying: "If any one would sue you and take your coat, let him have your cloak as well"; and "If any one strikes you on the right cheek, turn to him the other also." When they heard words like these, Jesus seemed no longer a worthy preacher of reform but a foolish dreamer and a dangerous radical. They did not continue with Jesus.

Jesus drew great crowds in Galilee with his curative work as a physician. For several months his healing ministry threw a splash of sunshine on the gray walls of human misery. But when Jesus sought to show that releasing the body from pain did not redeem the spirit from sin, and began to talk about the Cross, the throngs turned from Jesus. It is so today. Hosts of people are attracted by Christ the physician. Numerous cults are capitalizing on Christ's principles of healing. But as a recognized leader of one of these cults asserted: "[Ours] has little or nothing to say about suffering, pain, or sorrow; little about sacrifice, the atonement, or salvation through acceptance of the cross." Certainly such a position stops short of the Kingdom as proclaimed by Christ.

How gladly many heard Jesus say, "Come to me, all who labor and are heavy-laden, and I will give you rest." But when he added, "Take my yoke upon you, and learn from me," that seemed an unpleasant restriction on personal liberty. And when Jesus declared, "If any man would come after me, let him deny himself and take up his cross and follow me." Well, that was too hard a saying for the crowds, and they turned away.

When Jesus saw the throngs leaving, he turned to the twelve disciples and asked, "Will you also go away?" Peter replied, "Lord, to whom shall we go? You have the words of eternal life; and we have believed, and we have come to know, that you are the Holy One of God." Hence when Jesus came to his Last Supper, he said to the faithful eleven, "You are those who have continued with me in my trials."

Yes, many listened to Jesus when they heard what they liked. Many came and still come to Christ as patrons go to a store. They pick out the promises which please them and the sayings which make them feel good. But if we would enter the kingdom of God, we cannot remain patrons of Christ, we must become his partners, taking his yoke upon us and learning of him by working with him, accepting his hard sayings as well as his pleasing ones. One test, then, of a Christian is continuing allegiance to Christ. As Jesus said, "If you continue in my word, you are truly my disciples."

The Hebrew lawyer accepted enough of Jesus' teaching that he was "not far from the kingdom of God." But he did not continue far enough to enter.

Note a second step which the scribe failed to take toward the kingdom of God. He was near enough to see the duty of loving God and his neighbor, but he did not go far enough with Christ to discover the depths of God's love for man.

He probably knew some of the psalms which sang of God's goodness.

> Bless the Lord, O my soul;
>
> . . . .
>
> and forget not all his benefits.

But God the great Giver afar off is not so heartwarming as God the Lover near at hand.

He could look up from the Judean hills and sing:

> O Lord my God, thou art very great!
> Thou art clothed with honor and majesty,
>
> . . . .
>
> who makest the clouds thy chariot,
>   who ridest on the wings of the wind.

But the God of nature has no arms to pick man up when he falls.

As a devout student of his Hebrew scriptures, he had very likely shared the longing of the psalmist when he cried:

> As a hart longs for flowing streams,
> so longs my soul for Thee, O God.
>
> . . . .
>
> When shall I come and behold the face of God?
> My tears have been my food day and night
> while men say to me continually, "Where is your God?"

But the God whom the psalmist and the scribe sought did not come forth to meet them as did the father of the prodigal son.

The Hebrew lawyer with his understanding of the commandments might have had the fortitude of Job to keep on trusting God through persistent suffering and calamities, because he too might have realized that God's greatness is too vast for him to question or explain. But would he have come through his agony able to say with Paul when his thorn in the flesh remained, that he could hear the Lord say to him: "My grace is sufficient for you, for my power is made perfect in weakness"?

No, the scribe would not have heard the comforting message which came to Paul, because between Job and Paul, Jesus lived; and the lawyer, unlike Paul, did not continue with Christ far enough to learn the gospel of God's grace. Paul never saw Jesus in the flesh, but he saw the reflection of him in lives made loving by contact with the Christ. He had been present at the stoning of Stephen, one of Christ's converts. As Saul of Tarsus, he saw Stephen refusing to curse his enemies and looking up into heaven with a radiant smile, saying: "Behold, I see the heavens opened, and the Son of man standing at the right hand of God." Saul began to wonder what secret Stephen had which could sustain him under such blows. The loving face of Stephen lingered in Saul's mind as he left Jerusalem for Damascus. And finally on the road the light broke on Saul's mind, and he realized it was the Christ who gave Stephen his invincible love.

The command to love God is cold counsel until our hearts are warmed by the feeling of God's love for us. This is the creative contribution to love made by Christ. "God was in Christ reconciling the world to himself." He transformed love for God from the push of duty into the pull of desire. "In this the love of God was made manifest among us, that God sent his only Son into the world so that we might live through him. In this is love, not that we loved God but that he loved us and sent his Son to be the expiation of our sins. Beloved, if God so loved us, we also ought to love one another." This is the dynamic of love which the Hebrew lawyer did not go far enough with Christ to learn.

Christ generates love for God by revealing him as a Father going forth to meet his wastrel son on the way back from the far country of sin. Christ's parables are luminous with the love of God. And then he himself goes to the cross to demonstrate that "God so loved the world that he gave his only Son, that whoever believes in him should not perish but have eternal life." When we continue in Christ's words and life long enough, "being rooted and grounded in love, [we] may have the power to comprehend with all the saints what is the breadth and length and height and depth, and to know the love of Christ which surpasses knowledge." Then we are filled with the fullness of God and his love. Then the command to love God, which the lawyer knew, becomes an inner compulsion of the heart, known to those who are in the kingdom of God.

Also, Christ gives new dynamic to the second great commandment, "You shall love your neighbor as yourself." He charges our minds with the truth that God loves every individual, however obscure, unattractive, or sinful. Muretus, a Christian scholar of the sixteenth century, fell ill while on a journey. Some doctors were called in to treat him. They did not know him, and as he appeared unprepossessing, they said, "Let's try an experiment on this fellow, for he looks of no importance." From the shadow of the bed came the patient's voice, "Call not any man cheap for whom Christ died." In that remark is embedded a principle which makes human life worth more along the Mississippi and the Thames than along the Yangtze, the Volga, and the Ganges. (Even as I am writing this I read a letter to the *New York Times* by Father George Ford, pointing out the disparity in human values between the United States and the Soviet Union as illustrated by the latter country's infliction of capital punishment for certain crimes against property.)

When we think how much God loves each of his children, we begin to realize how much he suffers when sorrow or pain comes to them, and this begets a more sympathetic and understanding feeling toward them. Your neighbor's boy may seem a pest, but if he gets hurt and you see how his injury breaks the hearts of his parents, your heart melts too. Similarly Christ helps to generate brotherly love by transference of God's love. He creates a kind of family spirit embracing our neighbors, even our enemies.

Lucian, a brilliant pagan critic of the second century, laughed at the early Christians as silly innocents because they made sacrifices for other Christians even though they did not know them. Ah, that was a distinguishing mark of the Christian spirit. They loved others not because those others were lovable or congenial, and not merely because the law commanded love for neighbors, but because Christ had loved all of them enough to die for them.

At the Last Supper Jesus said to his disciples, "A new commandment I give to you, that you love one another." Why call that a new commandment? Had not the Hebrew scribe quoted from the law, "You shall love your neighbor as yourself"? But we see the newness when we read the rest of Jesus' statement at the Supper: "Even as I have loved you, that you also love one another." This last is what the lawyer had not learned. He was "not far from the kingdom of God," near enough to know that he ought to love God and his neighbor, but not close enough to realize how much God loved him and his neighbor.

The lawyer lacked a third element which belongs to those in the kingdom of God. He did not go far enough with Christ to feel the lift which comes from the consciousness of God's love. If we assume that he was a sincere seeker and not a mere heckler—and I do—then his question reveals a heaviness of heart felt by many devout Jews in their effort to keep the Hebrew laws. There were over six hundred commandments in the Hebrew code. To keep them all seemed almost impossible. Obedience was morally and mentally wearying.

To be ever aspiring proves exhausting unless it is supplemented by inspiration. Aspiration glimpses the goal we want to reach; inspiration gives us the music to keep us marching toward it. A good parent tries to stir both in his child. The father who ever urges his boy toward better work but never encourages him with credit for his achievements leads the lad to despair until he says, "What's the use? Nothing can please the old man." On the other hand, the wise father also seeks to keep his son aspiring toward a higher goal but he inspires the boy with praise for the advances he has made. To be always looking at our shortcomings tends to make us shortwinded and even to stop running.

Jesus brought both aspiration and inspiration. He said to men, "You . . . must be perfect, as your heavenly Father is perfect." But it is worth noting that he was also called "the friend of sinners." He stirred a money-seeking publican named Levi with such divine discontent that the fellow left his lucrative job to become the disciple of Jesus named Matthew. Jesus also lifted the repentant Magdalene from the street where she had been threatened with stoning, removed the blush of shame from her cheek and sent her forth to sin no more.

Jesus did not merely say, "Follow me." The effort to follow Christ as a pattern may often lead us to despair. His perfection seems too high for us. We cannot attain unto it. Why keep on trying? It was with reference to these religious burdens that Jesus spoke the words: "Come to me, all who labor and are heavy-laden, and I will give you rest."

Jesus did not say in substance: "Here is the law. Now go out and do as I tell you." Jesus said: "Take my yoke upon you, and learn from me." He teamed up with his disciples. A good and wise mother yokes herself with her little daughter, so that the child learns by trying to keep step with the grown-up, thereby getting both the direction and the tempo of the doing. Yes, the copying is so blended with comradeship that the little one feels the contagion of encouragement.

So Jesus observed those who were wearing their nerves ragged, chafing at their restrictions, sometimes plunging ahead too fast, sometimes lagging back dispiritedly and stubbornly. And he said: "Take my yoke upon you, and learn from me; for I am gentle and lowly in heart." That did not mean that Jesus was slow and easygoing, without force and drive. It meant that Jesus had the steady pace of divine patience. It was his patient timing with God's pace that gave Jesus such serenity under stress. When the crowd cheered him, he did not rush recklessly ahead. When the crowd cursed him, he did not falter or hang back. When he stood before Pilate as the governor prodded him with questions and the crowd clamored for his blood,

Jesus' poise was unshaken. Knowing that truth was on his side, he could trust his cause to time.

The yoke of Christ is easy because it teams the wearer with One of unflustered temper and unhurried tempo, with One who takes his stride with the centuries rather than with the hours, with One who did not chafe at delays because he was confident of eventual victory.

And further, Christ's yoke lifts us with new strength. Augustine likened the yoke of Christ to the plumage of a bird, an easy weight which enables it to soar into the sky. And Bernard of Clairvaux exclaimed: "O blessed yoke that bears the bearer up."

Those who catch the spirit of Christ feel that their faith is a lift rather than a load. They do not just cast their burdens on the Lord, absolving themselves from all effort. They realize with Ben Franklin that the Lord helps those who help themselves. They apply the formula of Paul, "Work out your own salvation with fear and trembling; for God is at work in you, both to will and to work for his good pleasure." Those who enter the kingdom of God work hard for him and they feel the lift of God at work in themselves.

To live in the kingdom of God is to co-operate with him as the farmer does with the soil, to give God a chance to use his fertilizing and fructifying power in us to bring forth the fruit of the spirit— love, joy, peace, and their like.

Many so-called Christians are like John the Baptist and the Hebrew scribe in that they fail to co-operate with God at work in them. When Paul came to Ephesus, he found certain disciples who had been recruited by Apollos.

He said to them: "Did you receive the Holy Spirit when you believed?" And they said, "No, we have never even heard that there is a Holy Spirit." And he said, "Into what then were you baptized?" They said, "Into John's baptism." And Paul said, "John baptized with the baptism of repentance, telling the people to believe in the one who was to come after him, that is, Jesus." On hearing this, they were baptized in the name of the Lord Jesus. And when Paul had laid his hands upon them, the Holy Spirit came on them; and they spoke with tongues and prophesied."

This matter of receiving power from the Holy Spirit has a mystery about it, but it is a characteristic of man. Thinkers of all times have tried to define what makes man different in his very nature from other creatures. They have pointed to man's gift of reason, his use of language, his ability to make tools or to combine in social groups. But other animals can do all these things in some crude fashion. Ernest F. Scott has said that the distinctive thing about man is that he is in contact with a higher world. He has the power to worship. He can receive messages which come to him from the Spirit.

A man may be going about his daily round when a thought flashes in upon him. He cannot tell whence it comes, but it makes him look at all things in a different way. In a time of crisis or difficulty or despair, he feels suddenly strong. That is the power of the Spirit.

A person faces a day that is drab and dreary. Then a letter comes or a phone rings and the vision of some loved one looms in the mind, and the feeling surges through the soul that it is great to love and be loved. Such is the power of spirit.

George Frederick Handel, who had been ill and almost bankrupt, set himself to compose an oratorio. Later he told his friends that when he was composing the "Hallelujah Chorus," he could hear angels singing, and he only wrote down music to which he was listening. Tennyson told us that he wrote his poem "Crossing the Bar" almost without knowing it. The words came to him, he said, all in a moment. He never could be sure that they were his. Such is the power of the Spirit.

John Wesley as a student at Oxford pursued a regimen of moral discipline to cure himself not only of wayward acts, but even of idle thoughts. He tried to clear his conscience by coming to America for missionary work with the colonists and Indians in Georgia. But still anxiety gnawed at his heart. Then one night in a little prayer meeting in Aldersgate Street, London, he heard read some words of Martin Luther interpreting Paul's doctrine of justification by faith. Wesley felt his heart "strangely warmed" by the conviction that Christ could save him. And he became endued with such power that he changed the religious mood of England in the eighteenth century. He had received the Holy Spirit.

The Hebrew scribe evokes our praise and our sympathy. He was "not far from the kingdom of God," not nearly so close, of course, as the heroic prophet John the Baptist. Like John he saw the laws of God, but he did not feel God's love and lift. We leave him standing somewhat as Thomas Hardy stood, listening to the caroling bird and wondering what made it sing.

V. AN EYE TO THE VITAL

In a drop of sea water under the microscope can be seen the elements which make up the ocean. Similarly Luke lifts to view a little scene in which is revealed a vast sea of experience. It is the visit of Jesus to the home of Mary and Martha, mentioned in the tenth chapter of Luke's Gospel. Martha appeared to be running the household. It speaks of her as receiving Jesus "into her house." Her sister Mary sat and listened to Jesus' teaching while Martha busied herself with the household duties. Our sympathy inclines toward Martha as she says to Jesus, "Lord, do you not care that my sister has left me to serve alone? Tell her then to help me." But Jesus answered her, "Martha, Martha, you are anxious and troubled about many things; one thing is needful. Mary has chosen the good portion, which shall not be taken away from her."

Mary had an eye to the vital. It has been said that in every situation the most basic question is not, "What must one do?" but "What must one do first?" When we have settled what has priority we are on the way to a solution. The first requisite of successful living is to know what is most vital. William Butler Yeats once defined genius as the art of living with the major issues of life. Certainly leadership in any line of endeavor involves the ability to distinguish the main point from the side issues and then to drive to the heart of the matter. When a good executive is called into a tangled situation, he singles out the essentials and brushes aside the secondary.

W. H. P. Faunce, president of Brown University, gave a chapel talk a generation ago on the subject, "Is It Worthwhile?" He recognized that it is increasingly hard to divide all possible acts into the absolutely right and the absolutely wrong. Hence, he advised his students to shift the query and try for one month to ask of each possible action not, "Is it right?" but "Is it worthwhile?" He said: "For one month divide all actions into the relevant and the irrelevant, the things that count and the things that do not matter, and see how simple life becomes. Is this really a big and worthy task to which I am giving my days and nights, or is it a petty mass of trivial details?" [1] A thing may not be wrong in itself, but if it consumes time which could be spent for something better, it becomes wrong.

We are almost in as much danger from loss of perspective as from loss of conscience. We must of course be watchful lest we surrender to open evil. But we must also beware lest we be gradually submerged in the clutter of fairly good things that do not matter.

In ordinary times when things are running smoothly with us, we live pretty much on the principle of first come, first served. Our desires reach out to seize their gratifications without much thought of grading them. Thus the good may keep out the best, and our days may become filled with sawdust like a child's doll.

But if an emergency, such as a war, confronts us, then we discover that some things have the right-of-way. The government may step in and designate priorities. Some of us can remember the days of war-time rationing, when we were told how much gas and soap and steak we could buy. In dictator-ruled lands today the people are not free to work just when they wish, go where they please, eat what they like. But in our country we are limited in the satisfaction of our desires almost solely by our power to pay. The question confronting us is, Can we of our own free will determine the objects for which it is worthwhile to spend our money and labor? Can we determine priorities in peace as well as in war?

This calls for perspective on the planning of our lives as well as

[1] *Facing Life* (New York: The Macmillan Company, 1928), p. 145.

on the organizing of our monthly budgets. Are we to go on spending our lives to secure our little piles of possessions, which the winds of adversity can blow away like chaff? Are we to struggle along, fretting ourselves to keep ahead of our fellows, fighting with other men and nations for prestige and power, and finally be frustrated by disappointment and death? Is there not some better way of planning life? Are we not wise enough to see what is worthwhile?

This call comes to us not only as citizens of a free country but as followers of Christ. Paul opens his letter to the Philippians by saying, "It is my prayer that your love may be more and more rich in knowledge and all manner of insight, enabling you to have a sense of what is vital." (Moffatt.)

This sense of what is vital was one of the distinguishing marks of Jesus, which merited for him the title of Master. It appears in many places. It is revealed in his visit to the home of Mary and Martha, where he found the latter flustered and anxious over her manifold duties. He said to her: "Martha, Martha, you are anxious and troubled about many things; but one thing is needful. Mary has chosen the good portion."

When Matthew compiled Jesus' sayings in the "Sermon on the Mount," he cited this:

Therefore do not be anxious, saying, "What shall we eat?" or "What shall we drink?" or "What shall we wear?" For the Gentiles seek all these things; and your heavenly Father knows that you need them all. But seek first his kingdom and his righteousness, and all these things shall be yours as well.

Here is Jesus' principle of priority.

We think of him that day at the well of Jacob, when a Samaritan woman came to draw water. Engaging her in conversation, our Lord discovered that she was trying to cover up the deep sins of her life with shallow comments. She sought to shift the conversation to all sorts of topics. But Jesus kept bringing her back to the point of her own transgressions until finally her sullen spirit surrendered and she went away a changed woman.

When we stand face to face with Jesus of Nazareth, there is something about him which calls us back to the central issues of life. We cannot shift his gaze off to the evils of the world; he makes us look at our own sins. We may point to our rich possessions, but he makes us ask ourselves what are they really worth. We may try to escape his gaze by busying ourselves with all sorts of activities, perhaps some of them are good deeds—but his eye keeps following us with the question, What is our main job? That is why a prayer in Christ's name in the morning gives poise and direction for the day. Christ reduces our complex living to its simple essentials. He keeps alive our sense of what is vital.

Consider first how Christ directs our eye to the vital in our individual lives. He said: "Your eye is the lamp of your body; when your eye is sound, your whole body is full of light." What does Jesus mean by a sound eye? Presumably he means the possession of simple, undistracted, unclouded vision, the ability to see things in clear focus and true light. The King James Version reads: "If therefore thine eye be single, thy whole body shall be full of light." Singleness of eye is a factor in clarity of mental vision. The trouble with too many of us is that we try to see too many things at the same time. We try to look in so many directions all at once that we do not see clearly the duty immediately before us. Our vision is darkened and confused by side glances. We look over the fences to see whether others are faring better than ourselves, and thus we cloud our minds with the shadows of envy. We look to the side to see if our rivals may be passing us, and then we stumble or lose heart. But when Christ gives us an eye single to God's glory, then we are freed from the side glances which confuse us with comparisons, confound us with jealousies, and dishearten us with the seeming successes of evildoers.

And this singleness of eye which Christ gives leads to a singleness of aim. In trying to keep up with Jesus, we cease trying to keep up with the Joneses. We turn our backs on yesterday's yelping pack of hounding worries and proceed on the principle of the apostle Paul when he said, "One thing I do, forgetting what lies behind and straining forward to what lies ahead, I press on toward the goal for the prize of the upward call of God in Christ Jesus." Christ comes into a personal situation somewhat as a good lawyer comes into a complicated legal case. Just as the lawyer reduces the various points involved to a few central issues and keeps these ever before the judge and the jury, so Christ singles out the essential issues in any perplexing problem and keeps them ever before us. As the Epistle of John puts it, "We have an Advocate with the Father, Jesus Christ the righteous." Christ, like a good lawyer, cuts away the confusing irrelevancies and keeps us to the main issues of living. Of course, the epistle's primary emphasis here is on Christ as "the propitiation" for our sins by his atoning death. Nevertheless, Christ did not have to soften God's heart, for God is love. Christ had to soften our hearts and show what we can expect of God. He said: "Whatsoever you ask in my name." Christ guides and sifts our prayers.

And when Christ gives a singleness of eye and a singleness of aim, he imparts a new surge of power. Yonder is a youth whose life seems at odds and ends. He has been going around in circles and tangling himself up in knots. He has been wasting his energies in wayward exploits and wasting his father's money in foolish ventures. Then he is gripped by some dominant purpose or a great love. And he straightens out like a garden hose when the strong current of water is turned on. We see his vagrant impulses unite to give him force and effectiveness. We say that he has found himself. When we get our eyes focused on what is vital, and our steps headed toward it, we get a new vitality.

And while we are speaking of Christ's giving us an eye to the vital, we ought to look with him closely enough to see what he means by being vital. We Americans need to be on our guard against a misconception of this over-worked word "vital." Vitality is frequently confused with vehement action. A person may have lots of vitality and yet keep still. Martha was active with her pots and pans; Mary sat quietly listening to Jesus. But the difference in activity was not a measure of their vitality. We deem it high praise to say of a man that he is "a live wire." The aliveness of a wire, however, is not measured by its sputter and sparking. Live wires are safe and effective when they are well insulated and silent. The measure of a live wire is how strong a current it carries.

Similarly with a person, his vitality is measured by the light-giving and life-giving power which he carries—yes, and keeps carrying. Some persons have tremendous drive and vitality for a time, but their energy slackens. The excitement of war arouses men to stupendous effort, but one tragedy of war is that it leaves so many burned-out hopes and bombed ideals. The love of one's work may call forth unflagging zeal, but retirement comes, and what then? A person may give himself to some objective with enthusiasm, and then comes disillusionment and he cries, as did Cardinal Wolsey after his abandonment by King Henry VIII,

> Had I but served my God with half the zeal
> I served my king, he would not in mine age
> have left me naked to mine enemies.[2]

Eventually we have to retire from our life work, but we never have to retire from Christ. Eventually death separates us from the earthly presence of our loved ones, but who shall separate us from the love of Christ? Shall tribulation, or peril, or famine, or nakedness, or the sword? Nay, not even death. For "in all these things we are more than conquerors through him who loved us."

The issue of what is vital becomes more imperative as life becomes more complex. Some years ago Sinclair Lewis, in a novel, brought an American traveler home from Europe and had him stand on the balcony at New York's Grand Central Station before returning to his home in the West. As this American looks at the crowd moving from ticket windows to train gates, it reminds him of a giant anthill

---

[2] William Shakespeare, *Henry VIII*, Act III, sc. 2, l. 455.

whose motivating principle seems to be, "Going somewhere, going quickly and going often." The people in the station crowd seem dwarfed into insectlike smallness. And the question rises in his mind, "Why is it that these individuals look so petty while the worshipers whom I saw in the great cathedrals of Europe did not seem so dwarfed?" And he concluded that there is something about men at worship which gives them a significance not given by mere motion in a crowd.

Man is made for something more than merely "going somewhere, going quickly and going often." Where are we going? Why are we going? What is the meaning of all this motion and commotion? Mere busyness is not progress. Mere employment is not prosperity. Mere production of goods is not goodness. Almost a century ago Disraeli said that the European ᴛalks of progress because by the aid of a few scientific discoveries he has established a society which has mistaken comfort for civilization.

And the ability to single out the essential becomes ever more important as life becomes ever more complex. This point is being stressed by certain contemporary writers, perhaps by none more effectively than by Thornton Wilder. In his *The Woman of Andros,* Wilder pictured a young man looking into the future. The young fellow had come to the conclusion that most mortals merely endured the slow misery of existence. That feeling was strengthened by the fretful attitude of his parents. And as he looked from their careers to his own, he began to analyze his future. He was twenty-five and that, he thought, was no longer young. He would soon be a husband and father. He would soon be the head of a household. He would soon be old. Time would have flowed by him like a sigh, with no plans made, no rules set, no strategy devised that would have taught him how to save those others and himself from the creeping gray, from the too easily accepted frustration. "How does one live?" he asked the bright sky, "What does one do first?"

And in the rush of our infinitely complex living Wordsworth's lines ring true:

WHOM CHRIST COMMENDED

The world is too much with us; late and soon,
getting and spending, we lay waste our powers.

In the 1960 election to the Hall of Fame for Great Americans there were over two hundred nominees for this highest mark of greatness. The College of Electors, consisting of 140 of our most eminent contemporaries, elected three, the first being Edison and the second being Henry David Thoreau. It seems of noteworthy significance that along with Edison, whose inventions have made the world so immeasurably more inviting and dynamic, should be chosen Thoreau, who withdrew from the world because he thought, with Emerson, that "things are in the saddle, and ride mankind." It would seem that the electors desired to combine honor to the inventor of useful things with honor to the thinker who saw the danger of things overshadowing men.

Thoreau withdrew to his cabin in the woods at Walden Pond to think. He saw the danger of improved means to unimproved ends. We remember at the time the Atlantic cable was laid Thoreau is reported to have remarked that it was thrilling, yes, but he supposed the first news to come over it would be that Princess Adelaide had the whooping cough. Thoreau was deemed worthy of America's highest honor because he believed that it is more important to have something worthwhile to say than to have improved means of saying it, more important to have worthwhile objectives than to have speedier conveyances, more important to increase manpower than to multiply horsepower.

In the spring of 1961 the *New York Times* asked ten men to answer the question, "What is the world's greatest need?" More than one cited the need of clearer and more adequate goals. General Maxwell D. Taylor, former Chief of Staff of the United States Army, wrote:

The need for recognized goals has never been more clear than now. A large part of the human race has lost its freedom to a handful of ruthless leaders of real energy and singleness of purpose, who are completely certain as to their aims. Whatever we may think of the evil of their actions, there is no trace of decadence in their dedicated pursuit of ends which, if achieved, will bury us even as Khrushchev has promised. Can we of the free world be equally sure of the ends which we pursue?

VI. WHAT IS WASTE?

In many ways we are manifesting growing concern to reduce waste. The constant speeding up of our tempo of living makes us increasingly averse to wasting time. The mounting governmental budgets and taxes awaken us to the dangers of wasting money—at least in some quarters. Industrial efficiency and competition are reducing the waste of human labor in drudgery and duplicated effort.

Yet with all our talk about eliminating waste, how wise and successful are we? Let us look into the nature of waste. And let us do it through the words of Jesus as they were called forth by a familiar incident near the end of his earthly life.

In the tense days between his "triumphal entry" and his arrest, Jesus is believed to have spent his evenings among his friends in the suburb of Bethany. One day he was dining with his disciples in the house of a man named Simon. Matthew and Mark describe the occasion in almost indentical terms. While the guests were at table a woman entered with an alabaster jar of very expensive perfume and poured it on Jesus' head. The identity of the woman is not clear. Luke in his account calls her "a woman of the city, who was a sinner." John's Gospel reports that the woman was Mary, the sister of Martha and Lazarus. Her name does not matter. It is her deed that made the dinner memorable.

Matthew records that when the disciples saw the woman anointing Jesus with the precious perfume, they were indignant saying, "Why this waste? For this ointment might have been sold for a large sum, and given to the poor." The Fourth Gospel asserts that it was Judas who criticized the woman's deed as wasteful, not because he cared for the poor, but because he was a mercenary thief. The rebuke of the woman's conduct, however, would be quite understandable as coming from any or all of the disciples for they had lived with Jesus long enough to catch his sympathy for the poor and his condemnation of waste.

The first feature of the woman's gift which caught the attention of the disciples was the *extravagance* of it. It was expensive. Mark reports that its cost was three hundred denarii (or pence). Some expositors estimate this amount at about sixty dollars in our money, but at least equal to four times that amount in first-century purchasing power. A $240 gift of perfume would indeed seem extravagant. Of course, such monetary measurements are rather futile reckoning because the scale of living in lush, modern America is difficult to compare with that of barren, first-century Palestine.

Jesus condemned the principle of living beyond one's means. He bade his followers count the cost before beginning undertakings, lest they be like the man who began to build and was not able to finish.

Yet while it is a sound business principle to live within our income, there are some areas of life where we cannot operate with our eyes on the balanced budget. Love is such an area. A father and mother should try to balance the family budget as to items of rent, food, clothes, entertainment, and the like. But they cannot budget the items of time and love and sympathy. If little Mary falls sick, mother does not say, "I'll see what time I can afford to give her." Nor does father say, "I'll figure out whether I can afford to get a doctor." There are times when love takes precedence over financial prudence.

Or suppose a young man is considering an engagement ring for his fiancée. He could say to her, "Let's be practical. My income is limited, and when we start housekeeping we shall need a refrigerator. So instead of wasting my money on a ring, I thought I would save it for something we can use." Ah, to a girl a ring on the hand is worth two refrigerators in the future! And, if it is true love, she will prize that ring to her dying day. There are times when life rises from arithmetic into love.

The anointing of Christ with the precious perfume was extravagant. It was a gift beyond the woman's income. But she was so grateful that she did not count the cost. She gave the best she had. And that is the feature which helped to make the value of her gift.

Think what it does to a mother's heart when her little son gives her the best apple in the sack or the best piece of candy in the box. How it would take the edge off her happiness if she discovered the little fellow keeping the best for himself and palming off the poorest on her.

Or think of a daughter looking back over her mother's life and saying: "Yes, mother was efficient. She counted the cost of everything. She gave us the time and thought and care which she could afford. She made both ends meet." What damning with faint praise! What keeps us hugging a mother's memory to our hearts? It is those days when she did not count the steps in looking after our welfare, those nights when she did not count the hours in watching by our beds of pain, that sacrificing of her own comfort and health to give us happiness.

And what is "the best portion of a good man's life"? Wordsworth says it is

> His little, nameless, unremembered acts
> Of kindness and of love.

In the anointing of Jesus we behold a grateful woman demonstrating a love that goes beyond the budget. And it is this extra costliness which gave her deed its value. If she had come in, taking out a few coins and counting what she had left, her act would have called forth no criticism from the disciples, but neither would it have warmed Jesus' heart as did her deed. My imagination tries to picture Jesus' face at that moment. It must have been suffused with tenderness.

Jesus appraised that woman's gift, not by the money which might have been gotten out of it in the market place, but by the love that went into it.

With all our wisdom of prudence, with all our business efficiency, let us remember that love is not wasteful when it gives the best it has. It is only in giving its best that love demonstrates its depth and sincerity. This principle applies in the family, in friendship, and in the worship of God. It was true insight which impelled the early Hebrews to give to the Lord the finest of their flocks and their fruits. God does not desire for himself the best of what his children have; but like any true father, his heart is warmed by the desire of his children to give their best. Likewise, Jesus was made glad by the woman's desire to give her best. Hence, the pouring out of that precious ointment was not waste.

We turn now from the cost of the woman's gift to the *spirit* of its giving. Since she spoke no words—at least none that were recorded— we can only conjecture as to her motive. If, as Luke says, she was a woman of the city who had been a sinner, she may have been making this gift in gratitude for her experience of salvation through Christ. If she was Mary, the sister of Martha and Lazarus, she may have poured out this costly ointment in gratitude for what Jesus had done for her family.

Jesus must have been looking at the spirit of her deed even more than the manner of it when he said: "Why do you trouble the woman? For she has done a beautiful thing to me. . . . In pouring this ointment on my body she has done it to prepare me for burial." From Jesus' words and from the general setting we can be pretty sure that she did what she did not out of charity or self-interest.

The woman was not a rich friend dispensing charity to a poor carpenter. If her motive had been charity she would have sold the perfume and given the money to him. And she was not seeking favors from him if her act was, as Jesus said, an anointing for his burial. Probably she surmised that he would soon be killed. Yes, her deed, as Jesus said, was "beautiful" because it was motivated by pure love and gratitude.

When we are concerned about waste, we must consider motive. We Americans are wasting millions in our giving today, not because we are giving too much, but because we give with the wrong spirit and motive. This is seen in both our individual and national giving. I believe that as Americans we should support our government's foreign aid program. It is our patriotic and our Christian duty to help other nations develop better living conditions. But millions of our dollars are wasted because they result in the wrong reactions.

Self-respecting individuals and nations resent being regarded as objects of charity. We must, therefore, keep our gifts free from the taint of pride and pity. We, in comparatively prosperous countries, should be so humbly grateful for God's rich bounties to our land that we want to share as equals before God with other members of his family who have received unequal material blessings. The spirit of good will and charity cannot flow between individuals or nations or races as a stream flows from a higher to a lower level. It must move as the tide moves across the ocean, that is, on the level drawn by the attraction of a Power above.

There is a basic difference between compassion and pity. Compassion is the feeling of sympathy between equals. In compassion we make another's misery our own. Pity is a feeling that flows from the strong to the weak. There is the suggestion of a stoop in our attitude toward those we pity.

In the King James Version the Latin word *caritas* is translated "charity." "Charity suffereth long, and is kind; charity envieth not; charity vaunteth not itself, is not puffed up . . . Beareth all things, believeth all things, hopeth all things, endureth all things." But we have so demeaned charity that the first definition now given in my dictionary is "liberality to the poor." And in that sense charity does vaunt itself, does get puffed up. We should restore the word charity to its Christian meaning of love by cleansing it of the spirit of condescension.

WHAT IS WASTE?

Some years ago an American diplomat stood with me at a window of our embassy in Moscow looking out at the Kremlin. He remarked that he believed the Soviet vocabulary had deleted the word charity. The Communists spurned the word. One reason, no doubt, is to be found in the condescending and contemptuous treatment accorded the poor peasants by the rich in the old Czarist regime. Sheer self-respect prompts people thus treated to cry, "We want justice, not charity."

And another cause for their scorn of charity could be found in the self-interest which poisoned the springs of the old Russian charity. The poor were given doles to keep them quiet. Hence today the Soviet Communists suspect the motives of any gift. The American representative was talking to me at the time of the Marshall Plan. The nobility of that gesture by America was wasted on the Russians because they thought we had some ax to grind. And all too often the motive of self-interest does tincture our charity.

Congressional appropriations for foreign aid can only be secured by the argument of enlightened self-interest. Perhaps that is the highest motive on which a government can give aid outside its borders, because it is responsible for those within its own territory and it must use the money raised by taxes for their welfare. Hence, the government must be convinced that its gifts to other nations also further the interests of its own citizens.

In giving aid to India or Burma or Pakistan, we not only help them but we also help ourselves, for their healthy economy means better business for us. But we must be sincerely concerned about their welfare if our dollars are to engender better relations. The people of other lands will respond to our gifts if they think we are really interested in their good, but they will lose respect for our aid if they suspect that we are using them as pawns against the Soviet Union.

Other countries have become so convinced that America gives in order to build bulwarks against communism that they pose and publicize the peril of communism in order to secure our gifts. Intelligent Jordanians have been heard to say that the United States does not give them a fair share of foreign aid because their little nation raises no threat of going Communist. And other lands have learned how to play the motive of fear on both sides of the line and bargain for favors from both Congress and the Kremlin.

The defect of enlightened self-interest is that it is never enlightened enough. It must be guided, redeemed, and supplemented by love. We cannot leave all foreign aid to governmental action, however enlightened its self-interest. There must be those, like that woman at Bethany, who give out of gratitude and love without calculating the cost or the reward. There must be the spirit which sent William Cary and Adoniram Judson and Bishop Thoburn to the foreign mission field—the spirit of sharing with others the blessings of Christ's gospel.

Nor can we leave all our needs for help in our homeland to organized charity. To be sure, charitable organizations have delivered us from the abuses of old-fashioned almsgiving. But the milk of human kindness cannot be delivered in corporate milk cans, however efficient the organization. We need those, like the woman at Bethany, who forget themselves in spontaneous generosity, who give because they are grateful and ask for no return, who lift the duty of giving into the beauty of giving and thus warm the heart of the receiver. Truly, as Jesus said of the woman who anointed him, "She has done a beautiful thing to me." The beauty of her deed was marred neither by the stoop of condescending pity nor by the taint of favor-seeking self-interest.

After seeing the cost of the woman's gift and the spirit of it, are we still asking, "Why this waste?" Let us follow the words of Jesus further: "Wherever the gospel is preached in the whole world, what she has done will be told in memory of her." This statement opens a vista which reveals the larger value of her deed.

The sheer, extravagant generosity of her gift makes it memorable. Halford Luccock contrasts those persons who pour themselves out in lavish self-forgetfulness with those persons who "always measure themselves out with a medicine dropper, frightened lest they spend a drop more than the legalities of the situation demand." Do we not know those whom he thus describes, little souls who are afraid to give themselves generously lest they give themselves away, calculating spirits who try to do a little drop of good here and a little drop of good there, but who never give themselves wholeheartedly and joyously? They are like the Pharisees whom Jesus condemned because they "tithe mint and dill and cummin, and have neglected the weightier matters of the law, justice and mercy and faith." The trouble with those who measure themselves out with a medicine dropper is that their righteousness is looked upon as medicine which the children of God do not like to take, whereas those who pour themselves out in generous goodness are loved and remembered.

And, as Jesus saw, the beauty of the woman's deed would go on being appreciated. To be sure, the perfume might have been sold for a sizable sum, which could have been given to the poor. But men are more than mouths to be fed and bodies to be clothed. The poor as well as the rich crave beauty. They have hungers of the soul. They have emotions to be stirred. To all normal beings, as Keats said, "A thing of beauty is a joy forever."

Christ Church, Methodist, New York City, was opened in November, 1933, when America was suffering a bitter depression. Bishop Francis J. McConnell spoke at the opening service. Bishop McConnell was known for his strong advocacy of social causes. The Christian church has supplied few, if any, better friends of the poor. Yet on that day of dedication he defended the use of the costly marbles and mosaics in Christ Church. He saw that the beauty of the building would go on feeding the souls of men down the decades, long after people would have forgotten the food which could have been bought with the money spent on the building. The creation of beauty is not waste.

Browning in "Abt Vogler" tells of an organist improvising. Suddenly he was inspired to give expression to a strain of music far better than he knew. He stopped, almost exhausted by the very ecstasy. But he could not recall what he had played. Try as he would, he could not recapture that wonder of sound. Was it therefore lost? No, Browning's organist declares his faith:

> There shall never be one lost good!
> What was, shall live as before.

A deed of beauty does not die. In God's providence a good is never lost. It shall live.

Yes, not only live but grow. As Jesus praised this woman for her beautiful deed, he seemed to be looking ahead down the centuries and foreseeing the future results of her generosity. As he predicted, the story of it has been told and retold, times beyond number, inspiring acts of love, melting cold hearts, opening closed purses. If we wish to measure the value of that perfume in Bethany, we must talk, not in terms of denarii or pence as did the disciples, but in terms of millions—millions of dollars given, millions of hearts gladdened. Was that really a waste?

If we are to understand waste, we must rise above niggardly, pinch-penny attitudes and catch something of the bigness with which God runs the business of the universe. The operations of nature often seem wasteful and nonproductive. Yonder is a plant full of pollen, yet only a fraction of that potential seed will ever come to fruition. When we look at nature's seeming wastefulness, we may become a bit like the young man who sat looking out over the Pacific Ocean. Not a ship was in sight. As he pondered the placid, majestic ocean domed by the glorious blue sky, he remarked to a friend: "Yes, it's beautiful, but I hate to see all that water out there doing nothing."

When we consider this matter of waste, we must change our method of measuring from utility to future fertility. Jesus told his hearers: "The kingdom of God is as if a man should scatter seed upon the ground . . . and the seed should sprout and grow, he knows not how. The earth produces of itself, first the blade, then the ear, then the full grain in the ear." But we in our rapid moving from the country to the city are losing the patience and perspective of the farmers Jesus knew. With our factories, our markets, our commercial methods, we think in terms of quick utility and man-made schedules.

Harold Phillips told of the little city girl who on her vacation in the country saw her first rainbow. As she looked at the colors against the sky, the little girl cried to her mother, "Oh, Mummy, what's it advertising?" And Dr. Phillips, in telling the story, added that the rainbow was advertising something that very much needs to be advertised; namely, those values in life which are of worth regardless of sale price.

If we cannot appreciate the beauty of rainbows and sunsets; of old masterpieces of art which are not for sale; of truth which is worth seeking for its own sake; of goodness which is its own reward—if we cannot see and enjoy the value of such things, then I fear we shall not understand the beauty and value of the perfume poured on our Lord.

We do well to be on our guard against waste. But what is waste? We hurrying devotees of the dollar look at generosity like this woman's, and we say, "Why this waste?" But is it waste to follow the promptings of love beyond the line of duty? No, it is such love that makes life worth living. Is it waste to spend time in prayer and worship? No, it is such practice that keeps the health of our spirits. Is it waste to spend money on beautiful churches and noble art? No, because man cannot live by bread alone. Is it waste to make sacrifices in the service of Christ?

Think of Jesus himself. When he left his Nazarene shop to become an unpaid itinerant teacher, his neighbors no doubt exclaimed, "Why this waste of a good carpenter?" When the crowds listened to Jesus' matchless words and yet did not mend their lives, and then when they later turned away, probably even the disciples were prone to cry, "Why this waste of all his work?" When Jesus, who might have saved himself, yielded to the fury of his enemies and went to the cross, Pilate, who could find no fault in him, very likely said to himself in bewilderment, "Why this waste of a good man?" But what seemed waste is what God chose to save the world.

VII. WHEN ARE WE LOST?

The story of Zacchaeus is familiar to us all. But how many of us are sure that we know the secret of Zacchaeus?

Jericho in Jesus' day was a thriving city. Through its crowded streets spread the news that Jesus was coming. Zacchaeus was the superintendent of taxes and very rich. He was eager to see this Jesus of whom he had heard so much. So he ran ahead and climbed a sycamore tree because he was small of stature. When Jesus came to that point in the street, he looked up and said, "Zacchaeus, make haste and come down; for I must stay at your house today." The publican was flattered, because with all his wealth, Zacchaeus was despised by his countrymen for being a tax gatherer, employed by the Roman overlords. The crowd showed its disapproval, but that did not deter Jesus from going home with Zacchaeus. After the visit the host came forth to announce that he would give half of his goods to charity and repay fourfold anything he had taken by cheating. Then said Jesus, "Today salvation has come to this house, since he is also a son of Abraham. *For the Son of man came to seek and to save the lost.*"

Such is the story of Zacchaeus. But the account bristles with questions. Why was the publican so eager to see Jesus? Was it mere curiosity? or an inner hunger? or the prick of conscience? Why did Jesus invite himself to the man's house? What did Jesus say to him in the privacy of the home which made the man disgorge his ill-gotten gains?

78

WHEN ARE WE LOST?

Lloyd Douglas in *The Robe* posed this last question. Marcellus, the central figure of Douglas' book, was asked what he thought Jesus said to Zacchaeus. Marcellus replied that maybe the Master said nothing. Perhaps Jesus just looked at Zacchaeus and he, returning the gaze, saw in the pupils of our Lord's eyes, the image of the man he might become.

While the meeting of Jesus and Zacchaeus leaves many questions unanswered, Luke's Gospel throws some light on the events inside and outside Zacchaeus' house, and especially on Jesus' words: "The Son of man came to seek and to save the lost."

The account of Zacchaeus is in the nineteenth chapter of Luke, but the preface to it is in the fifteenth chapter: "Now the tax collectors and sinners were all drawing near to hear him. And the Pharisees and the scribes murmured, saying, 'This man receives sinners and eats with them.' So he told them this parable."

In this parable and the two following it we have Jesus' answer to those who criticized his seeking contact with sinners like Zacchaeus, and in Zacchaeus we have a concrete situation illumined by the principles revealed in these parables.

The first story was about a lost sheep. "What man of you having a hundred sheep, if he has lost one of them, does not leave the ninety-nine in the wilderness, and go after the one which is lost, until he finds it? And when he has found it, he lays it on his shoulder, rejoicing."

In the light of this parable we see one aspect of Zacchaeus' lostness. Jesus restored him to the flock, saying, "This man too is a son of Abraham."

Sheep in their moods are so much like people. They go along with their heads down, greedily nibbling at the grass nearest them, so seldom lifting their eyes to get their bearings. Thus they wander away from the flock or stray near some dangerous cliff. Then they suddenly hear a noise, look up, become frightened, run hither and yon in panic.

It is hard for city dwellers to visualize the frightened eyes of a lost sheep. But as a boy on the farm, I saw sheep get lost. Also, I had an experience of lostness as a lad of ten. I had gone with my parents on a trip to Niagara Falls and on to the city of Toronto. Engrossed with the shop windows, I had hung behind the family. Suddenly I looked around in the crowd and saw no familiar face. It was only a brief moment of panic and hardly worth mentioning.

But that trifling experience has given me a more penetrating insight into the truly serious plight of Admiral Byrd during his first stay in Little America, as he was exploring the region around the South Pole. One night he left his cave to look at some meteorological instruments and to get some exercise. Since the danger of getting lost in the Antarctic darkness was real and likely to be fatal, he set up a line of sticks in the snow to guide his return. But he walked beyond the line before he realized it. Suddenly he discovered his situation and could find no trace of a way back to his cave. He records that there came over him a sinking, sickening sensation, as he whispered to himself, "Now you're lost." Fortunately, he did find his way back before it was too late. It is hard for us in our well-lighted, well-warmed, sign-plastered cities to imagine the full terror of being lost in polar snow, with death by freezing lurking only a few moments ahead.

We do not feel in much danger of being physically lost. The figure of the lost sheep does not seem to fit us who feel so modern and smart. We think we know our way around. And no doubt so did Zacchaeus.

But what is it to be lost? Arthur Holt has said, "A man is lost when he cannot define his present or plan his future." After World War I the youth of America and the Western world were called the "lost generation." They had been caught in the maelstrom of the war and its jazz era aftermath until they had lost their sense of direction, meaning, and purpose. Their mood was reflected in a significant best-selling book, *Anthony Adverse.* Young Anthony grew up in the Italian city of Livorno. He was clever and skillful. He knew his way around very well. But when he was about twenty-one, he took a trip to Cuba. One night in Havana, an old trader says to him that he was a type—very practical, and yet always aware of the mystery of things. He tells him he has not yet made up his mind what the world is like, nor what he is, and unless he comes to some conclusion about himself and his world, he would be a mere wanderer. And that is what Anthony remained until, toward the end of the story, he seemed to find the clues of life's meaning in the career of Jesus Christ.

During the depression of the early 1930's a young man confided in me his feeling of confusion. He related that his earliest memories were those of cutting out war pictures of the first world conflict. Then he was sent to school in the hectic period of the 1920's with its emphasis on self-expression. He graduated from Harvard in 1929 at what seemed the peak of prosperity. That fall, the country was catapulted into a depression. Some two or three years later he said to me: "I have never lived through what you would call normal times. What I need is something to believe in, something to hold to." Like a lost sheep, that young man was seeking a shepherd.

After the Second World War came another sense of lostness. Our government did somewhat better by its youth in sending GI's to college and expanding channels of scientific studies. Churches enlarged their memberships and facilities. The 1950's rolled along seeking peace of mind through "inspirational" sedatives, beguiled by thinking that bigness is greatness.

But by 1960 our sheeplike mood began to be disturbed out of its herd-mindedness. Multitudes became aware that they had lost their direction and the meaning of life. Some youth openly rebelled against it all and became "beatniks." Some leaders of the press began publishing symposiums on our national purposes. President Eisenhower appointed a commission on goals to redefine our directions. The Fund for the Republic designated a study group to re-examine the foundations of American character. The 1960's began as the Searching Sixties. Truly, as the Prayer of General Confession says, "We have erred, and strayed from thy ways like lost sheep."

Zacchaeus was a lost sheep. He had greedily looked for the "best pickings." He had nibbled at the greenest blades near at hand. He had become a tax collector under the Romans. There was good money in that, but the job incurred the scorn of his countrymen. Having lost his social standing, he lived for what he could get, and he took all the traffic would bear. He worked his way up until he had become superintendent of taxes. But he now awoke to the sad fact that he was lost from his own flock.

The sense of belonging is even more vital to us than the possession of belongings. A family may purchase the finest residence in the town. The house may be furnished in luxurious fashion. But if the family is not taken into the fellowship of the community, it is not happy. Its members would give their precious belongings for the privilege of belonging. This desire to "belong" may in itself become a form of feeding one's ego. But while such an attitude perverts the principle, it does not disprove the truth that to belong is more important than to possess. A life, to be fulfilled, must have something to belong to.

Whether it was that haunting sense of lostness which made Zacchaeus climb up to see Jesus, or whether it was the contact with Christ which stabbed him awake, we do not know. But when Jesus did come into his house, Zacchaeus so repented the greed which had led him astray that he gave half of his possessions to charity and promised to restore fourfold his dishonest gains. He gave up part of his belongings to regain his sense of belonging. Then said Jesus, "Salvation has come to this house, since he also is a son of Abraham." Jesus, the good shepherd, brought Zacchaeus, the lost sheep, back into the fold.

When are we lost? When we have lost our sense of life's meaning and direction. When we have greedily sought the nearest gains and foolishly followed with heads down the easiest way until we have become separated from the divine Shepherd and the people of God. Christ comes to seek and to save us by leading us back to God out of the lostness and loneliness of our sinful separation.

Turn to the second parable which Jesus used to illustrate lostness—

the lost coin. He said: "What woman, having ten silver coins, if she loses one coin, does not light a lamp and sweep the house and seek diligently until she finds it?" And then she rejoices. In the same way, said Jesus, the angels of God rejoice over one sinner who repents.

A lost coin has to be sought for. It cannot find itself. Jesus must have had this point in mind when he was explaining to his Pharisee critics why he went to dine with publicans and mingle with sinners. For this reason he invited himself to Zacchaeus' house. "The Son of man came to *seek* and to save the lost."

Some years ago, at a union Lenten service in Detroit, the prayer was offered by a Negro minister. In the course of his petition were these words: "O Lord, leave us not to ourselves." The vast underdeveloped and uncommitted populations of the world hold the balance of power in the current cold war which threatens to become global conflict. It is imperative that these be reached by the godly people who try to serve them before they are further exploited by the selfish interests which wish to use them. We need a quick, sweeping, sincere revival of Christian missions to seek the confidence of the newly formed nations and rising races and save them from conflict and chaos.

And how is it with ourselves? We may not think we are lost like lost sheep or lost souls. But do we know what coins of the spirit we have lost? We know when we have lost money, but do we know when we have lost the richness of our natures? We know when we have lost a loved one, but do we know when we have lost our lovableness? We know when we have lost our health, but are we aware when the cancer of pride is gnawing away at the purity of our motives? The Son of man came to seek and to save because we need him not only to find us when we are lost, but also to find what we have lost and to reveal to us our loss.

If the Christian church were to recover Christ's emphasis on seeking, it would revitalize its work of saving. If the church would seek more insistently and intelligently to discover the desires of youth, it would do less denouncing of juvenile delinquency and more adjusting to the rising tide of expectations sweeping through the younger generation. In the area of mental health we would give less attention to the abnormal seekers who come to our clinics and more help to the normal persons who need guidance but are too reserved to ask for it. In our concern for the aged we would seek useful activity and not merely economic security. If we would fulfill Christ's mission, we would seek to save the strong for service as well as to save the weak from sinning.

The tragedy of a lost coin is that it is out of circulation. It has lost its use. That was in part the tragedy of Zacchaeus. He was not using his talents. He cheated his countrymen not only by overtaxing them, but also by underserving them. He was able, as was shown by his rise to the superintendency of the tax collectors. But he was lost to the service of his people.

A little more than twenty-five years ago the Mayo brothers gave a great foundation for medical research to the University of Minnesota. The gift was accompanied by a letter from Dr. William Mayo in which he said:

Every man has some inspiration for good in his life—with my brother and myself it came from our father. He taught us that any man who has unusual physical strength, intellectual capacity, or unusual opportunity holds such endowments in trust to do with them for others in proportion to his gifts.[1]

Jesus sought out Zacchaeus to bring his unused and misused talents back into use. Zacchaeus was a valuable lost coin waiting to be found and restored to circulation for God and his people. "The Son of man came to seek and to save the lost" who can be put to valued work in the world.

When Jesus answered those who criticized him for dining with publicans and sinners, he told the parables of the lost sheep and the lost coin, and then added a third, the parable of the *lost son*. This

[1] Helen Clapesattle, *The Doctors Mayo* (2nd ed.; Minneapolis: University of Minnesota Press, 1954), p. 330.

story of the prodigal son is probably the greatest of all Jesus' parables. The details of the parable are embedded in the memory of Christendom. They need not be retold here.

When we think of the prodigal son we picture a fellow in rags and filth. The rich Zacchaeus does not fit that pattern. But surely Jesus had more in mind than material poverty when he pointed this parable. Winston Churchill, the novelist, in his book *The Far Country,* portrayed the prodigal's loss of standards and ideals as the most significant aspect. A prodigal is one who wastes any part of his life. When Charles Darwin confessed that in his single-minded application to his scientific pursuits he had allowed his spiritual faculties to atrophy, he was admitting his prodigal wastefulness. A financially successful person may neglect his spiritual resources until he "lays up treasure for himself and is not rich toward God."

Like the prodigal and like Zacchaeus a normal person is born with a divine patrimony. As Wordsworth wrote in his "Ode on the Intimations of Immortality":

> Trailing clouds of glory do we come
> From God, who is our home:
> Heaven lies about us in our infancy!

Little children feel very close to God. They talk to him almost as naturally as to their grandfather. And then so often,

> Shades of the prison-house begin to close
> Upon the growing Boy.

Very often he grows up in a home where God is not mentioned or counted on, except perhaps as a Being who will punish his wrongdoing. God is not thanked for food at the table. Thus the heavenly Father fades into dim unreality. To be caught praying is as embarrassing as to be overheard talking to oneself. And when we speak of God in church we do so in pious, unnatural tones. Thus we modern prodigals, however rich and well fed, get away from our heavenly Father in a "far country."

As long as life moves along smoothly, we may not miss God very much. In fact, we may think ourselves emancipated from some old-fashioned fears and restrictions. We may cease for a time to feel the pricks of conscience. But we cannot close our minds tight against the longings for something more than the world gives.

Thomas Hood was a poet and punster. He knew how to make the world laugh at its fears and foibles. Yet with all his comedy, there is sadness in his voice when he writes:

> I remember, I remember,
> The fir trees dark and high;
> I used to think their slender tops
> Were close against the sky:
> It was a childish ignorance,
> But now 'tis little joy
> To know I'm farther off from heaven
> Than when I was a boy.

Yes, in the midst of our daily activities, however engrossing they may be, there come those interludes of deeper thought when we feel a homesickness for "God who is our home." We may not clearly diagnose it or define it. But at least at Christmastime we catch the feeling that stirred in Chesterton:

> To an open house in the evening
> Home shall man come,
> To an older place than Eden
> And a taller town than Rome.
> To the end of the ways of the
>   wandering star,
> To the things that cannot be and that are,
>   To the place where God was homeless,
>   And all men are at home.[2]

---

[2] "Home at Last." From *The Collected Poems of G. K. Chesterton.* Used by permission of the publishers, Dodd, Mead & Company.

And then if some emergency comes or disaster strikes, the homesickness for God ceases to be a mild nostalgia and becomes an allconsuming desire. And we may cry with Job, "O that I knew where I might find him." In such times we want more than the God we see in nature, where "the firmament sheweth his handywork." (K.J.V.) We crave the kind of God Jesus pictured in the parable of the prodigal, a Father who seeks his lost son with an eye that can see him coming afar off and comes forth with compassion to welcome him home.

We do not know how long the prodigal was in the far country of wasteful indulgence before the famine came and he began to feel his desperate need. We are not told how old Zacchaeus was when he awoke to his hunger for something more than he was getting from his greedy life.

In Robert Louis Stevenson's story, *The Master of Ballantrae,* the young aristocrat was asked why he was such a rascal when he was so well versed in Scripture. He answered, "The malady of not wanting." Many of us suffer from the malady of not wanting God; some of us, because we do not feel the need of Him; others of us, because we do not want God putting a damper on our own desires. Augustine was a flagrantly worldly and licentious young man. He confessed that his prayer in his wild youthful days was, "O God, give me chastity and self-control, but not just yet."

But the seeking of our own pleasures after a while ceases to please. The prodigal wakes up in the far country of sin to a homesickness for his father's house. Sin always leads to alienation and loneliness.

A few years ago a man sat in my office. I had known him as a young man with bright prospects in his profession. With a good education and a lovely wife, he seemed to have an assured future. But he broke his home ties. He became estranged from his wife and former friends. My heart went out to him because I could see that the heart had gone out of him.

If I could have restored him to his job and reconciled him to his wife, I could have put him on his feet. But a good job, a good home, good friends are not enough to give the heart its full sense of at-home-ness. We put our heart into our work, but after a while we have to retire from it. We may put our heart into our homes, but in time homes are decimated by death. We cannot put our whole heart into the interests of this world, however good. Our earthly loyalties must be set in a larger at-home-ness. Only one Being is great enough to be the lasting home of the whole heart. That being is God—the God to whom the psalmist sang, "Thou hast been our dwelling place in all generations." That is why Augustine, after running the gamut of the world's pleasures, came at last to say: "Thou has made us for Thyself, O God, and we are restless till we find rest in Thee."

Zacchaeus was not poor and starving, but like the prodigal, he had become piggish. He had spent his energy and time in greedy grabbing. He had become a publican. That was an unpatriotic job which no Jew would take except for profit. And he had collected more taxes than he legally should. But when he confronted Jesus of Nazareth, he saw the swinishness of it all, and he said within himself, "I will disgorge myself of those disgraceful gains. I will give half of my possessions to charity and if I have defrauded anyone of anything, I restore it fourfold." Thus Zacchaeus arose and came back to the faith of his fathers, as a repentant son of Abraham. And Jesus said, "Today salvation has come to this house."

Like the prodigal, Zacchaeus came to himself. As a greedy publican he was out of character. He was not true to himself. Christ helped him to realize himself.

After the first fiasco of the Cuban invaders who attempted to unseat Castro, Walter Lippmann wrote in his column a message entitled, "To Ourselves Be True."

There are those who believe that in Cuba the attempt to fight fire with fire would have succeeded if only the President had been more ruthless and had had no scruples about using American forces. I think they are wrong. I think that success for the Cuban adventure was impossible. In a free society like ours a policy is bound to fail which deliberately violates our pledges and our principles, our treaties and our laws. . . . The American conscience is a reality. It will make hesitant and ineffectual, even if it does not prevent, an un-American policy. The ultimate reason why the Cuban affair was incompetent is that it was out of character, like a cow that tried to fly or a fish that tried to walk.[3]

Truly the American conscience is a reality for this is "a nation under God." We have inherited the spiritual traditions of the Judaeo-Christian faith. We as a nation are founded on biblical bases of right and wrong. We get away from home base at times and do reckless things, as did the prodigal son. We live all too often for greed and gain, as did Zacchaeus. But we cannot be content in loose living. The Son of man who died for us comes to seek us when we do things out of character.

The Holy Spirit is in us to disturb us amid our indulgence in "the far country" and to dispose each of us to "come to himself." And the living Christ is in our churches and traditions to call us back to a Father's house where love is waiting for us.

We recall Tennyson's poignant poetic story of Enoch Arden, the seaman whose prolonged absence convinced those at home that he had perished at sea. When at last he did return, he found his wife happily married. He stood looking through the window at the new family circle. He had returned too late. He would not break in on the one he loved. He went away to die in his loneliness.

The heavenly Father's home circle is never closed against a returning prodigal. The Father comes with open arms, joyously crying, "This my son was dead, and is alive again; he was lost, and is found."

"The Son of man came to seek and to save the lost."

[3] From the May 9, 1961, issue of the *New York Herald Tribune*. Used by permission of Mr. Lippmann and the *Herald Tribune*.

VIII. A MOST POPULAR SIN

Some sixty years ago Charles F. Aked, minister of New York's Fifth Avenue Baptist Church, declared that "the most popular sin in the world" seems to be ingratitude. By the term "popular," he meant prevalent rather than admired or well liked. Dr. Aked went on to say, "It is one of the worst crimes in the big, black catalogue of wrongdoing."

In his scathing denunciation of ingratitude, this modern Christian minister was in line with the Stoic philosopher Seneca, a contemporary of Jesus who wrote that ingratitude was, of all crimes, that which we account the most venial in others and the most unpardonable in ourselves.

The prevalence of ungratefulness may be proved on every hand. The Gospel of Luke, in the seventeenth chapter, gives one graphic scene which shows how common is this sin. Jesus was on his way to Jerusalem. As he entered a village he was accosted by ten lepers who stood at a distance and cried aloud, "Jesus, Master, have mercy on us." When he saw them he said to them, "Go and show yourselves to the priests." Jewish lepers would be required to report to the Temple priests in order to have their cure certified. And as they went, they were cleansed.

"Then one of them, when he saw that he was healed, turned back, praising God with a loud voice; and he fell on his face at Jesus' feet, giving him thanks. . . . Thereupon Jesus said: 'Were not ten cleansed? Where are the nine? Was no one found to return and give praise to

God except this foreigner?' And he said to him [the cured leper]: 'Rise and go your way; your faith has made you well.'"

Thus Luke reports a first-century Gallup poll of the ungrateful, and it ran as high as 90 per cent. It is doubtful that nineteen centuries have lowered that percentage.

Why is the sin of ingratitude so prevalent? Perhaps one reason is that it is not painted in such lurid colors as some other sins, like murder, theft, or adultery. The medieval theologians did not include ingratitude among the seven so-called deadly sins: pride, covetousness, lust, envy, anger, gluttony, and sloth. People do not think much about ingratitude as a sin, because they do not hear many warnings against it. This lack of public attention leads to much lack of gratitude. Many of us take benefits for granted without stopping to think whence they come, and even more of us do not think to thank our benefactors.

The boy away at school, who receives his father's money and his mother's messages without writing for weeks or months, very probably does not stop to think how heavy the hearts of his parents are made by his neglect. His is not a conscious, deliberate, premeditated form of cruelty. Hence, in considering ingratitude, allowance should be made for the feelings of gratefulness which do not find expression in words. Recently a father told how he was moved by his daughter's assurance that her long failure to thank him did not mean that she was not grateful. But even such mere thoughtlessness tends to make for the fact, as well as for the appearance, of ingratitude.

Also, ungratefulness may be due to lack of imagination. A young son or daughter leaves the parental home to make a living in the city. Engrossed in activities and pleasures, the youth does not take pains to picture how the parents, in some quieter place or perhaps on the shelf of inactivity, wait for letters. Deep in his heart, during his interludes of introspection, the son realizes his debt to father and mother, but he does not use imagination enough to appreciate the difference in outlook. Perhaps such neglect seems a rather pale sort of sin, but it bears resemblance to the inattention condemned by Jesus in his picture of the last judgment. A follower of Christ is expected to note human needs, and a thoughtful, decent, kind person does see them. ③ Moreover, ingratitude may spring from a lack of sensitivity. Some persons do not have the fineness of nature to appreciate the niceties of life and to feel the moods of others. A gentleman has been defined as one who never puts his rights before the feelings of others or his feelings before the rights of others. But the coarse-grained fellow is not likely to notice the little favors and courtesies accorded him by others or to feel the hurts and disappointments caused by his own failure to show appreciation.

Aesop sharpened this point in his oft-told fable of Androcles and the lion. The slave Androcles escaped from his master and fled to the forest. There he came upon a lion groaning in pain. At first Androcles turned to flee, but finding that the lion did not follow, he went back and found the animal's paw swollen and bleeding from a huge thorn. He pulled out the thorn, and was then sheltered by the lion in his den. Shortly afterward both Androcles and the lion were captured. The slave was sentenced to be thrown to the lions in the royal amphitheater for the amusement of the emperor. When the lion was unleashed, he rushed toward his victim whom, on nearer approach, he recognized as Androcles. Instead of devouring the slave, the lion licked his hands like a friendly dog. When the surprised emperor learned the story from Androcles, he released both the slave and the lion.

No doubt the story is familiar through the literary portrayal of it by George Bernard Shaw and others. But perhaps not so well known are the words which Aesop added to the fable: "Gratitude is the sign of noble souls." A fine nature feels grateful for the good will which lurks below the surface of so many ordinary, daily, personal contacts and for the unlabeled kindnesses which rise above the line of duty even in our hard competitive society. To little courtesies and considerations, and even to larger benefits, a coarse person is blind.

④ Yes, and ingratitude is due also to lack of humility. Many of us become so filled with a sense of our own importance that we take everything that is done for us as if it were our due. We think of our rights and what we ought to have, until even a sense of ill usage arises from the thought that the good conferred has been withheld so long. We develop a creditor complex, and many of us look upon others as owing us more than we are getting. We bemoan the poor values we get for our money. We denounce the government for the heaviness of our taxes, forgetting that, despite the extravagance and wastefulness of governmental organizations, most of us are not fully paying for the freedoms and securities we enjoy.

And as for our indebtedness to God, we are prone to forget about him in the midst of what we think we have done for ourselves. The early Hebrew lawmakers understood man's tendency to ingratitude. In the eighth chapter of Deuteronomy is this counsel to the pioneers of Israel: "Take heed . . . lest, when you have eaten and are full, and have built goodly houses and live in them, . . . and your silver and gold is multiplied, . . . then your heart be lifted up, and you forget the Lord your God."

This proneness to forget God as the giver of our blessings increases with the methods of modern living. More and more we are leaving the soil for the city, thus removing ourselves from the firsthand reminders of our dependence on God. Living and working amidst man-made things, we forget the forces of fertility. A scientist has figured that a farmer's effort is only about 5 per cent of the factors which produce a crop of wheat. We city dwellers eat the bread without thought of the 95 per cent which the Creator contributes. In fact, we seem to be ever less grateful to the farmers, and talk much about the farm problem. Thanksgiving Day sermons tend to deal less and less with God's bounties and more and more with governmental issues.

Instead of being humbly grateful to God and our fellow men for what they have done *for* us, we seem to be increasingly fearful and fretful about what men will do *to* us. In our self-importance we dislike to be reminded of our obligations, and hence we stop reminding ourselves. Many seldom pause to say grace at table and the practice of saying "thank you" seems to have less frequency and less feeling.

And if a person who has done us many favors should give some slight offense, we remember the injury and forget the past kindnesses. 5. Among the various causes of ingratitude, perhaps the most prolific is greed. Recall another of Aesop's fables. A wolf had been gorging on an animal which he had killed. A bone became stuck in his throat. He groaned and howled for help. At last a crane agreed to try. "I would give anything if you would take it out," cried the wolf. The crane put his long neck down the wolf's throat and pulled out the bone. When the crane asked for his reward, the wolf grinned and showed his teeth, saying: "Be content. You have just put your head inside a wolf's mouth and taken it out again in safety; that ought to be reward enough for you." At the end of the fable Aesop put these words: "Gratitude and greed go not together."

The greedy nature keeps the nose on the scent of the next desire and turns away from the fragrance of past favors. As soon as one want is gratified, another arises, and then another. In our rushing drive to get what we want when we want it, we have little time for recollection and less time for returning to thank our benefactors.

In the gospel record only one of the ten cleansed lepers went back to thank the healer. Probably present-day physicians could not testify to such a low percentage. Many of my medical friends show me generous gifts from their "GP's," their grateful patients. But when we survey in broad perspective the gratitude given in proportion to benefits received, perhaps Dr. Aked was right in calling ingratitude the most popular—that is, the most prevalent—sin in the world.

II. Having considered the causes of ingratitude, we now ask, Why is it so sinful?

It may seem a bit strange that Jesus should call attention to the nine lepers who did not return to thank him. He had taught that his followers should serve without looking for reward. He had counseled: "When you give alms, do not let your left hand know what your right hand is doing, so that your alms may be in secret." It was this principle of anonymous, unheralded, and unexpected giving which Lloyd Douglas developed into his best seller, *Magnificent Obsession*.

Certainly Jesus did not condemn the nine and commend the grateful one because he desired praise for himself. He was pointing to the basic iniquity of ingratitude. It is a trait which we abhor when it really becomes apparent to us. The ungrateful child who leaves his parents to poverty or suffering while he goes on to pleasure and comfort; the ingrate who accepts hospitality and help without any effort to repay; the fellow who receives the favors of a friend and says belittling things behind his back—such persons are despicable. Richard Brinsley Sheridan, in *The School for Scandal,* makes a character say: "When ingratitude barbs the dart of injury, the wound has double danger in it." What makes the deed of Judas Iscariot the symbol of sin's deepest thrust? It was that he had been the trusted recipient of Jesus' highest favors. We may rationalize Judas' act as his misguided judgment in trying to force Jesus to show his latent power, but the fact of his ingratitude remains. The adjective we usually link with ungratefulness is "base." We speak of base ingratitude that wounds the hearts of those to whom it is shown and poisons the minds of those who show it.

An ungrateful spirit vitiates the core of character. It opens the way to envy, malice, and all uncharitableness. And it closes the way to God because the Holy One dwells "with him who is of a contrite and humble spirit."

In a sense, gratitude is the source of religion in the soul. Only a grateful person really believes in God because he alone acknowledges God as the source of his life and being. Those who say that religion is born out of fear forget that human nature feels an ingrained necessity to give thanks at some times. Recently I was on an airplane when the captain announced that our landing gear was out of order. As we circled around for almost an hour, I felt fear. I prayed to God. We were told to put our heads down between our knees. I found that required more effort than when I was a boy, but the posture added to the intensity of my praying! When finally we came down to a safe landing, a surge of gratitude engulfed my spirit which was more truly religious than my petitions for safety when aware of peril.

There is the seed of gratitude in every human breast, however hardhearted. There is an impulse to be thankful, just as there is an impulse in the lark to sing. It may be muted. It may be neglected nearly to the point of decay. But it is there, and this seed of gratefulness must be cultivated if a person is to become healthy.

This fact raises the question how far Christ's cure went with the nine lepers in Luke's Gospel. It may be presumed that they were physically healed of their leprosy. What they did with their restored bodies we do not know. They may have gone forth to become publicans or highwaymen. But to the grateful one who returned Jesus said, "Your faith has made you well." The word "well" as used here may carry a connotation somewhat different from the word "heal," which is the usual Revised Standard Version translation of the King James Version term "whole." I have long felt that the word "heal" is not quite what Jesus meant by "whole." It may be noteworthy that the statement of Jesus to the leper is here translated, "Your faith has made you well." It would seem safe to assume that the mind and spirit as well as the body of the grateful leper had been cured.

Is a patient made completely well or really whole unless he does feel gratitude? Growing attention is being given to faith healing and psychosomatic medicine. We are coming to recognize more widely that mind aad spirit can exert healing power over some bodily ailments. We are increasingly loath to set limits to the spirit's potency. But are we giving comparable attention to the effect of restored bodily health on the spirits of men? The amazing advances in medical science and care have lengthened the span of life so that more millions of Americans are alive at sixty than ever before, and what is perhaps more interesting, they are more alive at sixty! But is the tremendous progress in physical healing making us healthier spiritually? Are people so grateful for their restored and lengthened health that they come forth from our hospitals and clinics praising God and setting themselves to serving their fellow men? Or do we turn to God for health and then go to the devil to spend it? When we are discussing how far faith can help in healing, we should also consider how much our healing is strengthening our faith.

Some time ago I was privileged to read a few letters from some grateful patients to their doctor. Hear these words from a little girl just old enough to write: "I want to thank you very much for being so good to me. I hope I was not too much trouble to you. . . . Please always remember me because I will always remember you."

Or read this note from a young father who apparently had been made cynical through being separated from his family by enforced military service. His baby daughter had been cured. He wrote: "It's good to know that we still have a few people in this world who believe in helping one's fellow man. If we had more people like that . . . then we wouldn't have so many young men in uniform away from home."

Is our health-seeking generation to go on like the nine lepers who were cleansed and then went their way without showing gratitude, or are we to be like the grateful one who came back and thus was made well both in body and spirit?

Gratitude is a visibly self-rewarding virtue. It makes for happiness. It inspires the mind with lively impressions and tends to beget an habitual cheerfulness unknown to those who have it not. If one should give me a pan containing sand with particles of iron mingled in it, I might feel for the iron with my fingers in vain. But if I took a magnet and swept through it, the bits of iron would be drawn out by the power of attraction. The unthankful heart, like my finger in the sand, discovers no mercies in the daily round. But let the thankful heart sweep through the day and, as the magnet finds the iron, so it will find in every hour some heavenly blessings—only the iron in God's sand is gold.

If gratitude is so necessary to health and happiness, how can it be cultivated?

One suggestion is a better use of the resources of memory. Contemporary Christianity has been emphasizing faith and hope to the neglect of memory. Our American go-getting spirit has affected our religion to the point that we have a spate of books prescribing how to use faith and prayer to secure future blessings of health, happiness, and prosperity. In our straining search for the blessings ahead, we use our minds for collecting but very little re-collecting. We might learn a bit of wisdom from the Persian vizier who is reported to have had in his palace a room called the "chamber of memory" in which he would spend an hour each day reminding himself how much he owed to those who had gone before him. Some time spent in grateful thinking of those who lived yesterday will help us in dealing with those who live today.

The psalmist sang of the divine Shepherd who "makes me lie down in green pastures," "leads me beside still waters," and "restores my soul." Left to ourselves, when we get into green pastures we go on so greedily eating that we do not lie down to digest what we have devoured. Maybe we could learn from the lowly cattle the value of chewing our mental cuds in meditation which enriches memory. With our modern means of communication and production, a man today receives more varied impressions in a day than did his grandfather in a month, but only those impressions which we assimilate really get under the skin and into the spirit.

Henry Nelson Wieman once suggested that, just as the devout Roman Catholic has a string of beads called a rosary to keep track of his prayers, so each of us should make a mental rosary of his most precious memories, including the beauty he has seen, the fellowship he has enjoyed, and the varied good gifts which life has brought. Of course we need no visible beads, but we should run over these memories and give thanks to God for each separate favor.

The suggestion has merit, for when we start to count our many blessings, "to name them one by one" as the rollicking old hymn put it, we begin to rummage among our memories and we uncover so many forgotten reasons for gratitude.

Our minds run back to the days of our childhood when parents sat beside our crumb-strewn beds and held our feverish hands. We think of their sleepless nights, their sacrifices and anxieties as they followed our wayward steps and forgave our willful acts. We recall the friends who stood up for us and went to bat for us when we were in danger of losing the game. We remember the teachers who, though poorly paid, took pains to guide our often unwilling minds.

Then we get to thinking about those who made this land a fit place in which to live. In early New England it was the custom at Thanksgiving to place five grains of corn at every plate as a reminder of those rigorous days in the Pilgrim Fathers' first winter at Plymouth, when the food supply was so depleted that only five grains of corn were rationed to each individual at a time. We do well to recall also that at the time the ration was down to those few grains, there were only seven healthy colonists to nurse the sick and that half their original number lay in the windswept graveyard on the hill. And yet the following spring, when the Mayflower sailed back across the Atlantic, only the sailors were aboard.

When our minds stir among our memories, we begin to feel deeply grateful for the blessings we take for granted in this land so "beautiful for pilgrim feet, whose stern impassioned stress a thoroughfare for freedom beat across the wilderness."

And when we start counting our mental rosary of blessings, our memories go back to the Christian church which through the centuries has been trying to lead us in the paths of righteousness and point the way to the life everlasting. And back of the church we see the Christ who laid down his life that we might live and who triumphed over death, thus demonstrating that goodness is too great for the grave. And back of the Christ is the heavenly Father who so loved the world that he gave his only Son to redeem us. When we sit down with the saints to comprehend the love of God in Christ which passes knowledge, its "breadth and length and depth and height," we too can feel something of the gratitude which came welling up in the heart of Isaac Watts and prompted him to write:

> Were the whole realm of nature mine,
> That were a present far too small;

WHOM CHRIST COMMENDED

Love so amazing, so divine,
Demands my soul, my life, my all.

If gratitude is to grow in our hearts we must cultivate the expression of it as well as the source of it. In my boyhood community we had a colloquial expression for courtship. It would be said, "John is paying attention to Mary." He paid attention to everything she did and said. He watched her at parties. He thought of her during the day and dreamed of her at night. Also he paid "attentions" to her. He wrote her letters. He sent her flowers and candy. (That was in the pre-Metrecal days!) Thus he came to win her affection and enjoy the romance of love.

Alas, the art of "courting" so slackens off after marriage. Husband and wife may remain loyal to each other. They may work for their mutual interests. They assume that actions speak louder than words. And they do. Words without works become "a noisy gong or a clanging cymbal." On the other hand, however, works without words can lose the music of their doing. A silent Vermont farmer on his golden wedding anniversary is reported to have broken into speech and to have said to his wife: "Sarah, I have loved you so much that sometimes I could hardly keep from telling you." Love can be kept like that for a long time in a deep freeze of silence, but it loses the rich flavor of romance. And the silence may prove tragic, as in the case of Thomas Carlyle, who loved his wife but did not appreciate the fine quality of her affection and did not express his gratitude for her rich contribution to his own work. After her death, when the tears of regret and sorrow gushed through his gaunt fingers, he cried: "If I had only known."

Recently a couple nearing the rocks of divorce reported to me their visit to a psychiatrist. He told them that they had been harboring their resentments. Suppose they had been husbanding their gratitude. Where husband and wife cultivate the art of expressing appreciation to each other, there is less likelihood of running to professionals for family counseling.

And the voicing of gratitude is as vital in our relations with God as with man. The psalmist repeatedly makes that clear.

> Bless the Lord, O my soul,
>   and forget not all his benefits.

> Praise the Lord!
> For it is good to sing praises to our God;
>   for he is gracious, and a song of praise is seemly.

The early Christian faith was nurtured in gratitude. Listen to Paul:

Let the peace of Christ rule in your hearts . . . . And be thankful. Let the word of Christ dwell in you richly, as you teach and admonish one another in all wisdom, and as you sing psalms and hymns and spiritual songs with thankfulness in your hearts to God. And whatever you do, in word or deed, do everything in the name of the Lord Jesus, giving thanks to God the Father through him.

Under the persecution of the first centuries the followers of Christ did not go about in a mood of complaint, pleading for pity and protection. They sang praises. They sang in prison. Even on the cross Christ's last words came from psalms heard in his youth.

Christianity has inspired more joyous praise than the other leading religions. Buddhism sings no hymns of utter joy. Its symbol is an idol that looks peaceful but impassive. Mohammedanism has little liturgy of praise. And George Buttrick asserts: "Incidentally, Protestantism has more outright thanksgiving than Romanism, as witness the hymns Luther sang before his conversion compared with those he wrote and composed afterward; for Romanism still trusts in part to man's works of penance, while Protestantism leans on nothing but the sheer grace of God revealed in Jesus." [1]

Note also that true Christians have discovered the deep sources of gratitude which physical sufferings cannot dry up. One of the most-

[1] *The Interpreter's Bible* (Nashville: Abingdon Press, 1952), VIII, 299.

used hymns of the Christian church is Martin Rinkart's "Now Thank We All Our God." That hymn of the seventeenth century was composed after a war, famine, and pestilence by a minister who had buried so many loved ones that by the world's tests he should have fallen victim to morbid bitterness. Yet hear him:

> Now thank we all our God
> With heart and hands and voices,
> Who wondrous things hath done,
> In whom His world rejoices;
> Who from our mothers' arms,
> Hath blessed us on our way
> With countless gifts of love,
> And still is ours today.

A person, a home, a nation, a church cannot be made "well" unless it be grateful. Our praying should have less pleading and more praising.

Ten lepers besought Christ to cleanse them. Only one came back to bless him. That grateful leper not only was made whole but his spirit has been a healing force through the centuries.

IX. THE DIVINE APPRAISER

When we picture Jesus in our imaginations, what are the most familiar scenes which come to mind? We see him, no doubt, as a boy in the Temple. We think of his teaching on the mountainside and calling little children to him. We picture him riding into Jerusalem and standing before Pilate. We see in our mind's eye the Savior with a crown of thorns on his head, struggling under the weight of his cross and then hanging from it.

But let us behold Jesus in a setting not sufficiently colorful to be portrayed often on canvas. It is described in the twelfth chapter of Mark's Gospel thus: "And he sat down opposite the treasury, and watched the multitude putting money into the treasury."

The room where he sat was probably in a portico of the Court of Women. Thirteen trumpet-shaped receptacles were provided, supervised by priests, and the donor had to declare the sum he was offering and the special ritual purpose for which it was intended. As Jesus watched there passed before him a procession of rich worshipers depositing their sizable contributions. Then came a poor widow. Her name and background are unknown. She put in two of the smallest Jewish coins in circulation. Yet with that small gift she stepped from the limbo of obscurity into the limelight of history. She became a symbol immortalized in the sermons of the centuries.

We would study her through the eyes of the divine Appraiser.

Jesus appeared utterly indifferent to money for his own use. There is no mention of what he earned as a carpenter, of what he received

103

as a teacher, of what he spent as a traveler. Jesus is never reported as asking for alms for himself, and the Gospels contain no treasurer's report.

Yet while Jesus seemed free from any personal concern about money, there is scarcely any subject to which he referred more often. Realist that he was, he recognized how the considerations of wealth are woven into the warp of everyday living. He lived among people who did not have much money, but the scarcity of it did not make them less eager for it. Jesus saw that the love of money can rival the love of God, and he declared: "No one can serve two masters, for either he will hate the one and love the other, or he will be devoted to the one and despise the other. You cannot serve God and mammon." In the words of an oriental proverb, "You cannot carry two melons in one hand."

And we live even more in the shadow of the marketplace than did Jesus' contemporaries. As we say, money talks. Many a writer designs his book in the hope that it will be taken up by Hollywood and then his profits will pyramid. But John Milton received for his masterpiece, *Paradise Lost,* five pounds down and fifteen pounds more in three installments on the sale of a certain number of copies. And the value of Shakespeare's plays is not measured by his royalties. Whenever a writer, an artist, a doctor, a minister, an artisan does his work with his eye on the pay envelope, he is likely to vitiate the quality of his work and to miss the joy of its doing. Some years ago the London paper *Tidbits* offered a prize for the best definition of money. This was the winning definition: "Money is an instrument that can buy you anything but happiness and pay your fare to every place but heaven."

Jesus, by his frequent references, sought to put money in its proper and secondary place. Recall his words in the twelfth chapter of Luke. A man accosted Jesus asking him to bid his brother divide the family inheritance with him. Jesus refused to adjudicate the case. Maybe there was merit in the man's request, but Jesus tried to lead the discussion into a deeper understanding of life's values. He said:

"Take heed, and beware of all covetousness, for a man's life does not consist in the abundance of his possessions." Then he proceeded to tell the parable of the rich farmer whose fields brought forth so plentifully that he had to pull down his barns and build larger. In his prosperity the farmer said to himself: "My soul, . . . you have ample goods laid up for many years; take your ease, eat, drink, be merry." But suddenly he died. And God said, "The things you have prepared, whose will they be?" And Jesus added, "So is he who lays up treasure for himself and is not rich toward God."

In getting a proper attitude toward money Jesus, the divine Appraiser, would have us consider the *source* of what we possess. As the collection plates are handed to the ushers in many a church, the minister repeats the words, "All things come of Thee, O Lord; and of thine own have we given thee." But like so many words in our rituals, the repetition of them often takes away their force. We should pause to let those words sink in. The tourist in London should stop to ponder the words chiseled in the stones of the Bank of England: "The earth is the Lord's and the fulness thereof." It is so easy to preen ourselves on man's achievements, forgetting that back of all those are the life-giving power of the sun, the bounties of the good earth in soil and mine and sea, the electrifying and wave-bearing wonders of the air.

And as for man himself, whence comes the power of mind and body to use the gifts of the good earth? Consider one of the most seemingly self-created acts we can imagine, a singer singing his own composition. The theme is his own. The voice is his own. But who gave him that mind to dream, that heart to feel, that voice to use? Parents and teachers were involved in the preparation of these talents. And back of these is the artistic gift which came from the Creator.

Most of our property values derive from still more obvious contributions of other persons. There came to New York City in 1783 a young man named John Jacob Astor. He was the son of a butcher in Waldorf, Germany. He invested his small capital in furs. He traded directly with the Indians, peddling gewgaws among them and buying their furs at low prices. He extended his trade to the Pacific Coast and his ships prospered in the China trade. With all respect to the organizing genius of John Jacob Astor, could we say that by his own efforts he pyramided the value of the farm he bought here in Manhattan for $25,000 to its later value of some $500,000,000? No, it was the growth of the community as a whole which created the future value.

This is a point which the writers of Deuteronomy wished to drive home. In the sixth chapter they wrote to the children of Israel:

When the Lord your God brings you into the land which he swore to your fathers . . . with great and goodly cities, which you did not build, and houses full of all good things, which you did not fill, and cisterns hewn out, which you did not hew, and vineyards and olive trees, which you did not plant . . . , then take heed lest you forget the Lord, who brought you out of the land of Egypt, out of the house of bondage.

When we stop to appraise our possessions, do we not have to admit how much has come to us as unearned increment through the growth of communities and corporations? We have been the beneficiaries of the rights and privileges for which our forefathers fought and died. We hold our property because of the law and order established at immeasurable cost. So many of our possessions are due to the co-operation of others that we can understand something of the spirit which prompted Edward A. Filene, the great Boston merchant, to say, "Why shouldn't I give half my money back to the people? I got it from them."

It would be well to think more about the *contributions* of others to us and less about the *competition* of others with us. And when we Americans are prone to feel that other nations impose on us by asking us to bear the lion's share of financial support of international organizations such as the United Nations, we ought to remember how much of our ability to give is due to God's rich endowment of this land.

Let us give proper credit to American enterprise and efficiency.

We do not need much urging for that! But who endowed our American forefathers with the qualities of industry and foresight? Who inspired the framers of our government with respect for the rights of life, liberty, and the pursuit of happiness? We Americans should humbly see ourselves as stewards of vast God-given resources and remember that such wealth and power can only be entrusted safely to those who use them for God's purposes and God's children.

When General Eisenhower was being feted in England by our allies after the victory over the Nazis, he uttered in one of his speeches these words: "Humility must always be the portion of any man who receives acclaim earned in the blood of his followers and the sacrifices of his friends." A London paper printed that excerpt from Eisenhower side by side with Lincoln's Gettysburg Address. No comment was added or needed.

George Bernard Shaw defined a gentleman as one "who puts back into life a little more than he takes out." We might add to his statement also that a gentleman is one who feels that he never can put back into life all that he has taken out.

When a person gets this feeling of indebtedness, it affects his whole life. It makes him more intelligent and serious in the choosing of his career. It shows also in little daily attitudes. We should appreciate the contribution made by those courteous enough to thank others for little kindnesses, who are sensitive enough to recognize services beyond the line of duty.

Why do we stress this rather trite truth that life is a trust for which we should be thankful? Because there are so many ne'er-do-wells who think the world owes them a living; because there are so many thoughtless people who never give any concern to the source of their blessings; because there are so many smugly successful people who think that they are paying their full way; and because there are so many disgruntled people who grouse about the fact that they are not getting their money's worth. To be sure, we are not getting our money's worth at many points. To be sure, some of the income taxes paid this past year will be wasted in governmental laxity and red tape. But in the grand total most of us are getting more than we pay for.

We are the heirs of God and joint heirs with Jesus Christ. Whether we are ten-talent persons or five-talent persons or one-talent persons, we should remember that God gave us these talents. We hold them in trust. And we are to invest them as trustees of God.

Let us then follow Jesus, the divine Appraiser, as he turns from the importance of money and the source of money to the *use* of it.

While Jesus asserted that we cannot serve mammon, which was a general word for property, he did say that money could be made a useful servant. He told the parable of the dishonest steward who provided a future job for himself by reducing the obligations of his employer's debtors. The point of the story was that the lovers of God in their service of him should use as much energy and skill as the lovers of money use in their worldly enterprises. He said, "The sons of this world are wiser in their own generation than the sons of light."

In his parables Jesus appeared to recognize the right of private property. For instance, in his story of the great banquet he cited the excuses given by certain invited guests. One said, "I have bought a field, and I must go out and see it." Another said, "I have bought five yoke of oxen, and I go to examine them; I pray you, have me excused." Jesus condemned the making of such excuses, for these illustrate the way our concern for possessions causes us to miss the invitations of God; but he did not raise the issue of the right to own the field and the oxen.

Apparently recognizing the right to own property, Jesus sought to teach the proper way of using it. He dealt with men where they live and our lives have a necessary relation to material possessions. Everyone owns something. Even communism has not gone so far as to encourage community tooth brushes and collective hair combing! The relation of religion to business has to be considered, for business without religion becomes sordid, and religion without business becomes sentimentally divorced from daily living. Jesus, the master of life, would teach us how to master material possessions so that they become aids and not hindrances to our life with God.

When a speaker now refers to Hermann Goering, he almost has to stop and explain who he was. But twenty years ago Goering made daily headlines. As Hitler's chief of air forces, he plundered the art galleries and residential palaces of Europe. He brought his booty back to adorn his mammoth country place outside Berlin. Some of our diplomats who visited Goering's palace described the mélange of good art and cheap chromes which filled the place. He did not know the value of the things he possessed. Like the cynic described by Oscar Wilde, Goering knew the price of everything and the value of nothing!

Jesus had a sure sense of value. He simplified life by selecting the essentials and not troubling himself about the rest. When we study his life, noting what he lived for and what he lived without, we begin to see how relatively unimportant are so many things which we think are necessary to our living.

The little Main Street stores in the small county-seat town where I did my boyhood shopping were not very well lighted. When a purchaser was examining a piece of cloth, the clerk would often suggest that it be taken to the door in order to be seen by sunlight. Christ counseled men on somewhat the same principle. He bade them look at the things they had or wanted in the sunlight of God by viewing them at the doors by which they entered and left this world.

Recall how Jesus once set a child in the midst of the crowd and said, "Unless you turn and become like children, you will never enter the kingdom of heaven." Children do not have much sense of market values, but they have an almost uncanny sense of character values. A child can detect the false notes in a grown-up. Boys recognize genuineness and courage in character. Christ would have us take our desires, our tastes, our ambitions back to the door of our childhood and see how they look in the light of innocence and simplicity.

And Christ would have us test the values of our purchases and possessions by looking at them in the light of the door by which we leave this world. We have cited his parable of the wealthy farmer who was planning large barns for his growing harvests when suddenly he was awakened from his dream of affluence by the fact of death.

Some years ago I spent a night in one of Nazareth's second-rate hotels. I was pitying myself that I had to spend even one night in a place so lacking in modern comforts. Then I fell to thinking that Jesus lived there for thirty years in a far more primitive time and demonstrated the richest life ever revealed. And I asked myself, What are the necessities of life? Food, clothing, shelter? Yes, but to get these things in necessary amount does not require the cutthroat competition and fighting of our mad world.

What are the other things we cannot live without? Beauty, truth, goodness—these are the ultimate values of life. And faith, hope, love— these are the basic hungers of the soul. But these are noncompetitive possessions. I can enjoy peace of mind like yours without taking it from you. I can revel in a masterpiece of art without buying it and locking it in my house. When we sit down with Jesus and take an inventory of life's values and necessities, we see how independent they are of property titles and national territory. So much of the anxiety to get ahead of others, so much of the insane race to get ahead of other nations is due to our desire to possess wealth for power rather than wealth for use.

Several years ago when Albert Schweitzer came out of Africa long enough to accept the Nobel Peace Prize, he said that "man has become a superman" through the new atomic powers now at his disposal. But man suffers from a fatal imperfection in his spirit. He does not know how to put these titanic powers to constructive use. Hence, Schweitzer said, "We are becoming inhuman in proportion as we are becoming supermen."

In 1953 Washington University in St. Louis observed its centennial. Presided over at the time by Arthur Compton, Nobel Prize winner in physics, the university brought to its campus many leaders of science. But in planning the observance, the committee declared that in concentrating on the means, it was no less concerned with the values to which they should be directed. Therefore the university would consider such questions as these: "What is the basic character and problem of human existence? Can life as a whole be said to have meaning and purpose; if so, what is it? What things are most worth believing or hoping? What values deserve our supreme allegiance? What does it mean to be human in the fullest sense of the word?"

For what do we go to school and college? To learn how to make money and things? But the basic question is not how much money can we make, but how much we can make of our money.

Christ comes to put his finger on life's priorities, to show us the goals of life's journey, and to help us take the first steps on the road to "life that is life indeed." When we take time in the spirit of Christ to study life's pattern, we discover what is the real business of living.

In Dickens' "A Christmas Carol" the miserly Scrooge is confronted in a dream by the ghost of his dead partner, Jacob Marley. Marley, like Scrooge, had been hard and stingy during life. And now from the realm of the departed the spirit of Marley appears condemning himself and warning Scrooge against the fate that had befallen him. As the ghost wrings his hands and bemoans his shortcomings, Scrooge tries to console him with the remark, "But you were always a good man of business, Jacob." Whereupon Marley's ghost cries: "Business! Mankind was my business. The common welfare was my business; charity, mercy, forbearance, benevolence were all my business." Too late Marley discovered what his real business in life was.

Perhaps now we are prepared for the divine Appraiser's evaluation of the poor widow's two copper coins. From Mark's record we almost get the impression that Jesus was moved to excitement. "He called his disciples to him." Here was something worth noting. He said to them: "Truly, I say to you, this poor widow has put in more than all those who are contributing to the treasury. For they all contributed out of their abundance; but she out of her poverty has put in everything she had, her whole living."

People reveal most clearly their true mastery of money in the way they give. Here was a poor widow who put her whole living into her giving. In his praise of her, Jesus made clear that, in the eyes of God, the value of a gift is measured, not by its market price, but by its cost to the giver.

There is a vital principle involved here toward which we pointed in the case of the woman with the costly perfume. When we sacrifice to make our gifts, they take on value for the one to whom we give.

In the Old Testament the Hebrew worshiper was bidden to give the finest of his flocks and fruits to the Lord, not because the Lord was pleased by the thousands of rams and the rivers of oil, but because the heavenly Father, like earthly fathers, is pleased when his children desire to give him the best they have. Their sacrificial manifestations of love make glad the heart of God.

Moreover, gifts that cost sacrifice do good to the one who gives. We human beings are so made that we must give up things in order to be strong and healthy. This is the principle involved in Jesus' words: "I am the true vine, and my Father is the vinedresser. Every branch of mine that bears no fruit, he takes away, and every branch that does bear fruit he prunes, that it may bear more fruit." Our lives, like vines, are made productive by pruning. My parents did not accept the truth of the old adage, "Spare the rod and spoil the child." But there were times when my father felt that his growing son needed a trimming. He had various methods of vinedressing whose value I did not appreciate at the time, and whose effectiveness may not be visible in the present product. But the principle is valid. Our lives, to be healthy, must be pruned by sacrifice. We must give up some things we like if we are to grow up into the likeness of him we call the Christ.

If church members really grasped this principle of giving, it would work a revolution in Christian philanthropy. In our modern promotion of giving we measure from the wrong end of the yardstick. We fix our eyes on the amount to be raised and then seek the most painless way of extracting it from the possible givers. We cite the percentages of exemption allowed by the government for charitable gifts. We stress the motive: Why not give to a good cause since the taxes will take it anyway?

Also, like the rich whom Jesus saw casting their gifts into the Temple treasury, we give out of our abundance amounts which we do not miss too much. Our gifts to God so often smack of the spirit described by the prophet Isaiah in his ironical picture of the pagan idol maker:

He plants a cedar and the rain nourishes it. Then it becomes fuel for a man; he takes part of it and warms himself, he kindles a fire and bakes bread; also he makes a god and worships it . . . . Half of it he burns in the fire; over the half he eats flesh, he roasts meat and is satisfied; also he warms himself and says, "Aha, I am warm, I have seen the fire!" And the rest of it he makes into a god, his idol; and falls down to it and worships it; he prays to it and says, "Deliver me, for thou art my god!"

When we give to our religious faith and institutions only the residue of our goods after we have satisfied all our other wants, our gifts do not do much good either to the heart of God or to the health of our own spirits. We so seldom get out toward the frontiers of sacrifice where stood the poor widow whom Jesus praised.

Of course, most of us have never experienced the feeling of being down to our last farthing. Moss Hart, in his autobiography *Act One,* tells of his impoverished boyhood in the Bronx. He did hunger for better food than his parents could afford. But his little heart hungered for more. He tells of a night during the Christmas-shopping season when his father took him through booth after booth, asking the price of toys and other presents. The little fellow's heart would jump at the expectation of getting something he so eagerly wanted. But the father, unable to find anything which his few cents would buy, brought the lad home without a single present. In such bitter poverty the boy's starved heart did not have enough to live on.

But think of the poor lad's parents. Who suffered more, the boy longing for the presents or the father who saw his little son's brimming tears and could give nothing to solace his breaking heart? Life has its moments when we see clearly that "it is more blessed to give than to receive."

What became of the poor widow who passed through the Temple treasury we do not know. Her gift was too trifling to matter in the day's collection. But the heavenly Father who sees the falling sparrow takes note of the dropping coins. With him that gift counts most which costs the giver most. Her deed also caught the eye of the divine Appraiser, and she has become an immortal symbol of loving sacrifice.

X. WHEN RELIGIOUS FAITH COMES ALIVE

How real does Christ seem to us at this moment? We believe that a historic character named Jesus lived in Nazareth nineteen centuries ago. But is he a living presence among us now? Do we feel him beside us in our times of decision and sorrow? Does he make a vital difference in what we shall think and do tomorrow?

We try to make Christ real to ourselves by portraying him on canvas, by picturing him in glass and mosaic, by dramatizing him in sacrament and symbol. We use our imaginations to recreate an image of him as he walked among men. We thrill to the moving Negro spiritual: "Were you there when they crucified my Lord? . . . Were you there when they laid him in the tomb? . . . Were you there when he rose up from the dead?"

Well, suppose we had been there and had seen him with our own eyes, would we have appreciated Jesus Christ for what he was? Aye, more, would we have appropriated what he came to give us? We may see another person, even live near to him, and still be separate from him. We may be interested in him and admire his achievements and yet not feel any vital link with him.

Matthew Arnold, in speaking of England, wrote: "Greatness is a spiritual condition worthy to excite love, interest, and admiration; and the outward proof of possessing greatness is that we excite love, interest, and admiration." To Matthew Arnold, England was great because she inspired all three emotions. But how about our feelings toward Matthew Arnold? He still arouses our interest and admiration because of his literary attainments. But it could hardly be said that he kindles our love.

When we turn to Jesus, our interest is aroused by his inexplicable power of healing and his unparalleled triumph over the tomb. Our admiration is stirred by the wisdom of his teaching, the sinlessness of his character, and the courage of his conduct. But above all is the amazing love which he awakens in the hearts of millions who have never seen him in the flesh. Napoleon is reported to have pondered the fact that leaders like himself and Alexander the Great could command vast armies and inspire them with courage by their physical presence, but Jesus of Nazareth could reach across the centuries and hold the loyal devotion of followers who never saw him and yet would die for him.

When we come to love another person, that person becomes alive in us. And in this kindling of love, Christ is supreme above earthly rulers. When Sir Winston Churchill observed his eighty-fifth birthday, and more recently when he returned from the hospital after a serious accident, there was an outpouring of genuine affection perhaps unequalled by the feeling toward any other contemporary. But the love for "dear old Winnie" is limited by the postwar iron curtains and will be lessened by the passing centuries.

Nor does any other religious leader kindle the loving devotion accorded to Christ. Jews and non-Jews admire the mighty lawgiver Moses, but they do not sing: "Moses, lover of my soul, let me to thy bosom fly." Gautama Buddha is revered for the selflessness of his spirit and the sublimity of his thought, but his followers do not say to him what Whittier said of Christ:

> But warm, sweet, tender, even yet
> A present help is He;
> And faith has still its Olivet,
> And love its Galilee.

How does Christ generate life-giving love in other lives? Let us go back to his first disciples. Jesus had been conducting a very popular mission in Galilee. He had taught large crowds. He had healed many. He had fed five thousand in a most unaccountable way. But how were all these wonderful works affecting his hearers and disciples? Did they understand what he was trying to do? He would test them.

Mark records that Jesus turned and asked his disciples, "Who do men say that I am?" Matthew reports it, "Who do men say that the Son of man is?" They replied: "Some say John the Baptist, others say Elijah, and others Jeremiah or one of the prophets."

Let us pause to consider this first question and answer. Jesus was concerned to know, "Who do men say that I am?" Jesus did not need the favorable opinion of others to sustain his own self-confidence. He got that from God. But he did want to know how far men were comprehending his mission and methods.

And the disciples were concerned to know what others thought of this man they were following. They were sufficiently human to be affected by popular opinion. They themselves were simple villagers, and they wondered at his power and wisdom. But they were encouraged when they saw that the common people heard Jesus gladly. They were heartened when they heard their fellow listeners say that he spoke as one "having authority, and not as the scribes." The common people could see that Jesus was no mere scribe quoting proof texts from the Scriptures. They put him in a class with the prophets. Maybe some of them did not know that John the Baptist had been beheaded in prison and they mistook Jesus for John, the popular preacher who had been such a sensation along the Jordan. And some thought that Jesus was Elijah reincarnated. Elijah's career had been so dramatic that he was vividly remembered. And others thought this Nazarene carpenter and teacher was the prophet Jeremiah returned to earth.

It is noteworthy that to some Jesus suggested Elijah—ardent, enthusiastic, sometimes stern. And to others he seemed a Jeremiah, the prophet of the tender heart and tears. Jesus was such a blend of qualities that he defied analysis. He was the "light of the world" whose refracted rays produced a spectrum of personality's colors—mastery and charm, enthusiasm and tranquillity, remoteness and reachableness. He was God's perfect, all-inclusive man.

It was a tribute to Jesus that his countrymen classed him with the great Hebrew prophets. Rabbis frequently give high praise to Jesus as one of the Jewish prophets. Some may claim, as did the Jewish writer Klausner in his book *Jesus of Nazareth,* that throughout the Gospels there is not one item of ethical teaching which cannot be paralleled either in the Old Testament, the Apocrypha, or in the Talmudic and Midrashic literature of the period near to the time of Jesus.

But Klausner does admit that there is a note of originality in the Gospels because Jesus condensed and concentrated the ethical teachings in a more prominent way than in Jewish literature. And John Knox points out that Jesus demonstrates his originality as a teacher and prophet by the way his ideas are conceived and expressed.

Jesus was original in the warmth and abandon of his ethical teaching. However much sound advice the Old Testament may give on doing good to others, it was Jesus who said, "Whosoever shall smite thee on thy right cheek, turn to him the other also" (K.J.V.). The old Levitical law had bade men to love their neighbors as themselves, but Jesus said, "I say unto you, 'Love your enemies' " (K.J.V.). Where in the Old Testament can you find a parallel to the parable of the good Samaritan? And where can Jewish literature duplicate the parable of the prodigal son, for the point of the story is not only that the son wasted his substance, but that the father seemed to waste his love, pouring it out with utter lavishness on the boy who deserted him and dissipated his estate and broke his heart.

When the disciples reported that men said Jesus was one of the prophets, they were revealing that the crowd had not comprehended the whole truth. Jesus was a prophet and more than a prophet. There was an original force about Jesus' teaching. There was in him a power of personality greater than his preaching and his healing.

WHEN RELIGIOUS FAITH COMES ALIVE

Nineteen centuries have passed since Jesus put the question, "Who do men say that I am?" Those little oral reports which the disciples brought to Jesus have grown into uncounted volumes of opinion and testimony. Within a few years after his death there were many writings about him in circulation. The compilers of the New Testament sifted the books now in the canon out of a mass of current literature. The Bible has become the best seller so far outdistancing all other books that there is no need of comparison. Religious volumes pour from the press. There is no end to the books about Jesus.

And if our religious faith is to come alive in us we must listen to what others say of Christ. We give ear to the news of the world almost every hour on the hour. To hear the daily news of what men are doing without listening to the good news of what God in Christ is doing is as debilitating to our morale as it is for a political candidate to hear only his opponent's speeches. We should balance the news of what bad men are trying to do *to* us with the news of what God and good men are doing *for* us. When we open our minds to the good news of the Gospels and read what the first-century followers said of Jesus; when we learn what the people of our day are finding in Christ, then there begins to well up an awareness of Christ's living presence in the world.

The first-century Christians wrote, that they beheld the "glory of God in the face of Jesus Christ" (K.J.V.). We twentieth-century Christians can behold the glory of Christ in the faces of those who worship him. Up in New Hampshire is a cliff that in profile resembles the craggy brow and the sharp nose and the stubby beard of a man, and it is called "The Old Man of the Mountains." That resemblance was discovered by a hunter seeing the reflection of the mountain in Profile Lake at the foot of the cliff. We can catch the reflection of Christ in the adoring eyes of little children as they listen to a Christmas story, in the grateful eyes of devout sufferers as they hear his comforting words, in the reverential gaze of sincere worshipers as they sing his praise and pray at his altar.

Yes, we are led toward the appreciation of Christ by seeing crowded churches and strong men whom we admire bowing in reverence before him. And my mind is opened with wonder and awe toward Christ when I receive a Christmas card carrying these words:

Nineteen centuries have come and gone. And today He is the center of the human race and the leader of the column of progress. I am far within the mark when I say that all the armies that ever marched, and all the navies that were ever built, and all the parliaments that ever sat, and all the kings that ever reigned, put together, have not affected the life of man on the earth as powerfully as this one solitary life.

But Jesus was not content merely to ask what other men said about him. He asked a second question, *"But who do you say that I am?"* And Simon Peter replied, "You are the Christ, the Son of the living God."

If our religious faith is to come alive in us, we cannot live on the reports of what others say about Christ. We have to come to some conclusion about Christ, each for himself. Here Christianity makes a unique claim for Christ. We do not have to commit ourselves thus in regard to other historical characters. We can look objectively at Washington and say, "Some hold him to be the greatest president our nation has ever had; others consider him the fortunate creature of circumstance." Recently in South America we saw statues of Simon Bolivar on every side. Most people there hail him as the architect of Latin American liberty, but I read a book on the trip which pictures him as an ambitious adventurer. I did not have to take sides for or against Simon Bolivar.

But with Jesus Christ a unique claim is made. He is recorded as saying, "He who is not with me is against me, and he who does not gather with me scatters." That is a stupendous assertion, which to many seems an insult to their intelligence and mental freedom. Why do we have to take sides against or for Christ? Why can we not reserve our judgment and say, "Some hold Jesus to be a prophet, some think he was a poetic dreamer, some regard him as a great teacher. I cannot quite make up my mind"?

The way I understand Jesus' claim is this: He is, as Peter said, "the Christ, the Son of the living God." He incarnates the forces by which God runs this universe. We can no more be neutral toward the forces embodied in Christ than we can be neutral toward the force of gravity. Christ embodies the forces and laws of love and truth and goodness. If we go with his force of love, we gather; if we go against him, we scatter. Just as in the physical world there are two opposing forces, the centripetal which pull toward the center, and the centrifugal which hurl away from the center, so in life there is the gathering, Christ-like force of love and opposed to it is the scattering force of hate and fear. We must choose.

Let us not be misunderstood at this point. To say that we must choose for or against Christ does not necessarily mean that we must openly enroll under the banner of some church which bears his name. On one occasion the disciples came to Jesus and said, "We saw one casting out devils in thy name; and we forbad him, because he followeth not us." Jesus replied, "Forbid him not: for he that is not against us is for us." (K.J.V.) The issue was not what banner he carried, but what direction he was going, what motive was moving him. A man may be aligned with Christ and yet be a devout Jew or Hindu, Roman Catholic or Protestant. What counts is not the religious label but the love force.

It must be added, however, that if a person sincerely wants to align himself with the power of Christ, he must look to the means as well as the end. To conceal one's allegiance to Christ through fear is cowardice which disqualifies one from being his follower. To hold aloof from the church, which is the Body of Christ, because one finds no branch of the church that fully fits one's ideals is a sign of short-sightedness, narrow-mindedness, and pride. In a day when organization is necessary to the promotion of any cause, one must take hold of the longest lever available; and the Christian church, however imperfect, is the most potential agency for Christ's work in the world. And in a time when anti-Christian forces are pitted against the power of Christ on a global front, it behooves everyone who would "gather" for Christ to show his colors, stand up, and be counted.

Browning, in "Bishop Blougram's Apology," presses home the challenge which cannot be evaded:

> What think ye of Christ, friend? when all's done and said?
> Like you this Christianity or not?
> It may be false, but will you wish it true?
> Has it your vote to be so if it can?

It is not enough to catch the reflected glow of what the gospels and the poets and the martyrs have said about Jesus Christ. Who do you say he is? That is the question Jesus put to Peter. And Peter's reply was, "You are the Christ, the Son of the living God." Simon Peter, the uneducated fisherman, could not understand all the arguments of the scribes and Pharisees about Jesus. He did not fathom the historic teaching of Israel about a Messiah. But he had lived with this Nazarene carpenter for months. He had heard his matchless words and observed that his conduct matched his words. He had seen Jesus heal and had marveled at his power. He had felt the warmth of his love as he cleansed the lepers and held little children in his arms. He had heard Jesus say to sinners, "Thy sins be forgiven thee." Only God was supposed to forgive sins, but Jesus imparted a grace which enabled publicans and harlots to rise in newness and purity of life.

To what conclusion did Peter come? Was this Jesus a dreamer? No, his teachings were too wise and practical for a sentimental dreamer. Was he a charlatan claiming to be like God in forgiving sins and healing diseases? No, this Jesus did bestow grace and health. If he was not the world's cleverest deceiver, he must be divine. And Peter came out with his great confession, "You are the Christ, the Son of the living God."

We go on a third step to Jesus' reply to Peter. Mark, whose account is regarded as highly compressed, reports that Jesus "charged them to tell no one [about him]."

Jesus' request would seem to suggest that he was not ready to accept publicly the label of messiahship. Sherman Johnson in the *Interpreter's Bible* writes: "The gospel tradition shows that he was conscious of a unique vocation, so great and transcendant that none of the religious terms then in use was capable of expressing it. He knew that he was commissioned, with an authority greater than that of any prophet or king, to teach and lead the people of God."[1] If Jesus had permitted Peter to herald him as the Messiah, his work would then be expected to fit the pattern of the traditional Hebrew hopes. But Jesus felt the time had come "to show his disciples that he must go to Jerusalem and suffer many things from the elders and chief priests and scribes, and be killed." Jesus bade his disciples be quiet about the messiahship, for he was choosing not a crown but a cross.

Matthew goes beyond Mark and records Jesus as making a reply which has been the subject of much controversy. Matthew's account reads: "Jesus answered him, 'Blessed are you, Simon Bar-Jona! For flesh and blood has not revealed this to you, but my Father who is in heaven. And I tell you, you are Peter, and on this rock I will build my church, and the powers of death shall not prevail against it.'"

This is the statement on which the Roman Catholic Church rests its claim for the primacy of Peter among the disciples and the primacy of the Bishop of Rome as the lineal descendant by apostolic succession from Peter.

George Buttrick confesses the puzzlement of the honest expositor and raises some fair questions:

We must remember carefully both the late first-century date of this Gospel, and the church nexus from which it came. It was written in circles where the primacy of Peter was of major concern. Would James, brother of Jesus and leader of the church in Jerusalem, have agreed that vs. 18 was the mind of Christ? Would Paul, who looked with deference on the

[1] *Op. cit.*, VII, p. 448.

leadership of James (Gal. 2:9), have agreed? Would the Johannine circle have agreed? [2]

We shall not here pursue further the question of what sources Matthew had for enlarging Mark's account to include Jesus' assertion that Peter was the rock on which he would build his church. It is Jesus' praise in vs. 17 which interests me most and which seems slighted by the commentators.

Peter had just declared his conviction that Jesus is "the Christ, the Son of the living God," which is the central faith of the Christian church. Whereupon Jesus said, "Blessed are you Simon Bar-Jona!" Then he added as a reason for his blessing, "For flesh and blood has not revealed this to you, but my Father who is in heaven."

Peter's belief was not derived from the opinions of other persons. One characteristic of Peter was that he did not conform to any patterns of belief or behavior. He was original. Behold him in the impulsive things he did: jumping out of a boat to go to Jesus across the water, drawing up his feet when Jesus started to wash them, hacking off a servant's ear in the heat of anger, swearing that he never knew his Lord—always himself, whether admirable or blameworthy. Peter was an ardent, blunt man who blurted out what he thought and felt. His faith was firsthand.

Was not Jesus saying something more than that Peter's conviction came not as a secondhand derivative from other human believers? He was asserting that Peter's faith came not even from flesh-and-blood contact with himself, but from his "Father, who is in heaven." Humanity of itself can never discover God or find him out. The realization of God must always be God's own disclosure of himself in the heart of man.

However commentators may discuss Jesus' reference to Peter as the rock on which the church is founded, we can hardly dismiss Jesus' praise of the rock on which Peter's faith was founded. It rested on the revelation of the Holy Spirit. Paul bore witness to the sure foundation of such faith when he wrote: "And no one can say 'Jesus is Lord' except by the Holy Spirit."

Yet while Peter's faith in Jesus as the Christ was a gift from the Holy Spirit, he had reached the state where he could receive it by the exercise of his own faith. Of course, the faith that is in our natures from infancy is in itself a gift from God. As Pascal told us, we would not seek God if he had not already found us. Nevertheless, Peter was praiseworthy because he had struggled to keep the faith which Jesus had rekindled in him when he called him from his nets. Peter's fiery, impetuous nature had so many hurdles to overcome. Yet he held on. When the crowds began to desert Jesus, Peter stood by. No doubt, he was often bewildered by the turn of events. Probably he often said to himself, "I don't get it." But at last through storm and struggle, his faith had "got him."

So often we speak of "getting religion," as if it were a faith or a force to be attained by our own efforts. And then we stop before religion "gets us." The apostolic advice is: "Work out your own salvation with fear and trembling; for God is at work in you, both to will and to work for his good pleasure." So frequently we fail to keep on working until we feel God at work in us. Some persons have just enough religious faith to make them blush when they do wrong, but not enough to make them glow when they do right.

Peter must have blushed often at his blunders and failures. He has been described as a naturally timid man trying to be brave. But he struggled on until he felt "him who by the power at work within us is able to do far more abundantly than all that we ask or think." Then was revealed his faith in "Christ as the Son of the living God." which is the faith by which the church lives.

Peter was not made perfect by his faith. The dismal night was to come when he would deny that he ever knew Jesus. But that darkness would pass and Peter would be present to receive the counsel and promise of the risen Christ: "Behold, I send the promise of my Father upon you; but stay in the city, until you are clothed with power from on high."

Peter and the other disciples followed their Master's orders. They stayed in Jerusalem. They kept together. They talked over their Lord's promises. They lived again their experiences of his love and power. They communed with Christ in their prayers and meditations. They waited in expectancy of his return. They surrendered their wills to do their Lord's will as it should be revealed to them. And then on the day of Pentecost, when they were all together in one place, the divine Spirit descended upon them and they received new light and strength for their work. They were "clothed with power from on high." Pentecost became the birthday of the Christian church.

A wise observer of our time recently said that wherever we look we find able men doing good work, but we miss all signs of inspiration; that men work only for pay and then with the one desire to do as little as possible; that perhaps our chief need in these modern days is to recover that old belief in the [Holy] Spirit.

Certainly the Christian church can only be revived as it deserves the praise given to Peter: "Blessed are you, Simon Bar-Jona! For flesh and blood has not revealed this to you, but my Father who is in heaven."

XI. GOD'S GRADUATES

What would you reply if someone said to you, "You are my friend if you do what I command you"? I venture to think your first reaction would be resentment. It sounds almost arrogantly presumptuous for one person to say to another, "If you want to be my friend, you must do what I tell you." Yet the fifteenth chapter of the Fourth Gospel records Jesus as saying to his disciples, "You are my friends if you do what I command you."

There must be more to this statement than first meets the eye and ear. Let us look into the relationship which led up to these words.

The disciples had begun to follow Jesus as *seekers*. Some of them had observed Jesus walking and talking by the shore of Galilee. His personality attracted them. He appeared to have something which was lacking in their lives. His air of mastery, his calm confidence, his assurance of purpose betokened the possession of a secret which they would like to possess. So Simon and Andrew, Philip and Levi, and others left their work to follow Jesus.

Then they listened to his teaching. Jesus spoke words of such wisdom and beauty that the people marveled. They said that he spoke as one "having authority, and not as the scribes." So many of his sayings seemed so practical that they found them helpful in their daily living. Jesus' advice about overcoming anxiety and making friends with one's accusers seemed sound and down to earth. Also, the disciples must have been impressed by the crowds that flocked to hear Jesus in the first weeks of his popularity. Surely if so many others wanted to hear this Nazarene teacher, he must have something. So they followed seeking help from Jesus' teaching.

Moreover, they were amazed at Jesus' healing power. He made the lame to walk, the lepers to be clean, the blind to see. Simon Peter's mother-in-law was cured of a fever. Such crowds came to see Jesus heal that on one occasion a patient had to be let down through the roof to reach the hand of the healer. Even a member of the Sanhedrin named Nicodemus was so impressed that he came by night to learn the secret of this Nazarene's power. The disciples were swept along by the crowds seeking health at the hands of the great physician.

Also, they heard Jesus talking about eternal life. The disciples shared the prevailing belief that there is a life beyond the grave. But their concept of immortality was shadowy and unappealing. Jesus "brought life and immortality to light through the gospel." He portrayed God as a Father who is more eager to give good things to his children than are earthly parents. Jesus seemed to have such assurance about eternal life that he was not afraid of death. They, too, wanted to assure themselves of this indestructible life. They shared the longing of the rich young man who came running to ask Jesus: "What shall I do to inherit eternal life?"

Yes, the disciples followed at first with the crowds seeking the help and health and hope which they thought Jesus could give. But seeking did not make them friends of Jesus. Jesus was not deceived by the crowds which came after him. On one occasion he bluntly said to a large company which had followed him to the other side of the lake: "You seek me . . . because you ate your fill of the loaves." Genuine friendship is not formed on the basis of the benefits to be gotten. To be a mere seeker after Christ does not make one a Christian.

This is the consideration which is so disturbing in our contemporary religious situation. Since the end of the Second World War America has been experiencing an awakening of religious interest. Church membership has reached an all-time high. But thoughtful church leaders are aware that this increased interest in religion is not a proof of a real religious revival. Many persons may attend church, and even join the church, merely because they are seeking for something they want. And many a time the churches try to attract people by catering to their desires. Our lush material possessions and prosperity leave the souls of men unsatisfied, and the church offers religion as a recipe for finding what they are missing. Prayer is advocated as a way of getting from God the health, the happiness, the prosperity we crave. Religion has been popularized by stressing the promises of Christ and soft-pedaling his demands. Preachers have been told that if they would learn and practice Jesus' way of presenting their product, they could keep their churches full and their people contented.

Some preachers are prone to shape their methods of promotion through more study of public relations than of divine relations. And they devise some clever public announcements which do catch the eye. A few years ago during an epidemic of influenza in southern California I read the following church ad in the *Los Angeles Times:* "Avoid crowds and escape the flu, doctors say. Yet you want to attend church this Sunday. Then come to the least crowded church in Los Angeles." Then followed the name of the church.

But when we restudy the Bible we are reminded that Jesus did not keep his crowds. The multitudes who flocked to him seeking his boons turned away when Jesus began to talk about sacrifice and the cross. Jesus did not base his decisions on a Gallup poll of his listeners, nor did he found his church on a crowd of seekers. Hence, Bible-studying churchmen today are waking up to the fact that in our efforts to popularize Christ, we have not been proclaiming the whole gospel. And the results are beginning to show in lax morality and spiritual emptiness.

Listen to a secular voice, that of John Steinbeck. Returning to America after a prolonged stay in England, Steinbeck recently decried the cynical immorality of a country that has too much and doesn't know how to handle its good fortune; where the child in the typically prosperous family looks up from its bulging pile of Christmas gifts and says, "Is that all?"; where there is a "nervous restlessness, a hunger, a thirst, a yearning for something unknown."

Let us get this point clear: sound ethical religion cannot be based on mere seeking for the advantages to be gained from God. The crowds that followed Jesus to get his help were not his friends. But let there be no misunderstanding here: Jesus was a friend to them. The Pharisees even accused Jesus of being the friend of publicans and sinners. Friendship, however, is a two-way street. The mere seekers did not qualify to enter into friendship with Christ. A person may wish to be my friend, but I cannot become his friend by merely wanting what he wants to do for me.

In the century before Christ, Cicero wrote a magnificent treatise, "On Friendship," which has become a classic. In it Cicero said: "Friendship springs from a natural impulse rather than a wish for help; from an inclination of the heart combined with a certain instinctive feeling of love, rather than from a deliberate calculation of the material advantage it was likely to confer." [1] Then to illustrate the point Cicero cited his friendship with Africanus. He said:

Did Africanus want anything of me? Not the least in the world. Neither did I of him. In my case it was an admiration of his virtue, his opinion, maybe, which he entertained of my character, that caused our affection. Closer intimacy added to the warmth of our feelings. But though many great material advantages did ensue, they were not the source from which our affection proceeded.[2]

Cicero went further to assert that friendship grows by giving rather than by receiving. We are drawn more closely to a friend when we feel that we can do something for him.

Now if this be true—and I think a little second thought will corroborate it—then we are ready to move to the second stage in the relationship between the disciples and Jesus. They advanced from seekers to *servants* and *soldiers* of Christ. At first they had followed

[1] In the *Harvard Classics* (New York: P. F. Collier & Sons, 1914), IX, p. 18.
[2] *Ibid.*, p. 19.

with the crowds seeking what Christ could do *for them*. When the crowds began to dissolve, the disciples continued with Christ to see what they could do *for him*.

While Jesus was teaching in Capernaum, he laid down some pretty stiff requirements for discipleship, and many of his followers drew back and no longer went with him. Jesus turned to the twelve and said, "Will you also go away?" Simon Peter answered him, "Lord, to whom shall we go? You have the words of eternal life; and we have believed, and have come to know, that you are the Holy One of God." The longer the disciples continued with Jesus, the more convinced they were that he was the Christ.

When Jesus announced that he would go to Jerusalem again, his disciples, concerned for his safety, said: "Rabbi, the Jews were but now seeking to stone you, and are you going there again?" But they would obey him. Even Thomas, the most skeptical of the twelve, said: "Let us also go, that we may die with him." They were no longer following for their own sakes, but for his sake.

They heard Jesus talking repeatedly about the kingdom of God which he had come to establish. They did not fully understand it. They thought that it was to be some kind of temporal rule with officers. And they were human enough to ask who would be greatest. The mother of the sons of Zebedee came asking for the first two places for her sons. Jesus answered them: "You know that the rulers of the Gentiles lord it over them, and their great men exercise authority over them. It shall not be so among you; but whoever would be great among you must be your servant . . . ; even as the Son of man came not to be served but to serve, and to give his life as a ransom for many."

This was a revolutionary principle of social organization. But they did what we now ask those joining The Methodist Church to do; that is, they pledged their allegiance to Christ's kingdom, even though they did not fully comprehend its implications. They were no longer mere seekers after the boons of Christ the teacher and Christ the great physician. They were enlisted as servants and soldiers of Christ the Lord.

It is high time to recover this note of soldierly enlistment in the proclamation of Christ's gospel. My teen-age was over when the First World War broke out. In the churches of my youth we sang the rousing militant hymns like "Onward, Christian Soldiers" and "Soldiers of Christ, Arise." But two world wars have thrown such hymns into disuse, if not disrepute. The tragedy of war is that it not only slaughters its millions of God's children, but it also prostitutes so many godly motives. War calls forth some of our noblest qualities, such as heroism, honor, love of country, unselfish devotion and then uses them in the devilish business of debauching and killing. After we have seen what war does to the bodies and souls of men, we are almost afraid to sing:

> Onward, Christian soldiers!
> Marching as to war,
> With the cross of Jesus,
> Going on before.
> Christ, the royal Master,
> Leads against the foe;
> Forward into battle,
> See His banners go!

Such words, we think, sound as if the church sanctions war. And God forbid!

Christ was and is the Prince of Peace. He said to Peter: "Put your sword back into its place; for all who take the sword will perish by the sword." Yet Christ also said: "Do not think that I have come to bring peace on earth; I have not come to bring peace, but a sword." Those two statements are not contradictory. In the first, Christ was denouncing the use of the sword of steel; in the second, he was calling for the use of the sword of the spirit. As I understand him, Christ called for men to use as much heroic courage and sacrificial devotion in fighting against war as men now use in fighting their wars.

Christ called his followers to enlist under his banner in fighting for peace and brotherhood.

Some years ago the president of Wellesley College was telling me of the transformation which took place on her campus during the First World War. The girls forgot their personal rivalries and petty concerns and joined wholeheartedly in those activities which were supposed to aid the war. The president said the scene was beautiful to behold if one could forget the shadow of war. Then she asked if I thought we could ever develop such enthusiastic co-operation of effort and spirit in peacetime for peaceful purposes. If we cannot do so, we shall never end war.

And there are hopeful signs of such growing unity. The great body of Protestants in the United States, more than 35,000,000 are enlisted in the National Council of Churches—and also in the World Council of Churches—while only some small groups are attacking these. It should be added that one large denomination which is doing splendid work in many places is also outside the National Council of Churches, but many of their leaders co-operate.

To be sure, large religious organizations may say and do things with which the individual Christian may disagree. I hold no brief for all the pronouncements of the National Council of Churches and the World Council. I have respect for those sincere Christians who honestly fear that the church may be infiltrated by subversive influences. But I have no respect for those professional profiteers who have found how profitable it is to play on the suspicions and prejudices of people. As long as there is money to be made by appealing to people's fears and hates there will be demagogues to do it, and the church is not free from them.

Yet the Christian church is not so divided as many press reports might lead some to think. The growing spirit of co-operation among the Protestant churches during my forty years of ministry is so amazing that I would say the Christian church is today engaged in the struggle for social decency, civic righteousness, and international peace on more fronts and in more movements than ever before.

Let us revive some of our old fighting hymns and sound again some of the heroic notes of our Christian faith:

> Soldiers of Christ, arise,
> And put your armor on,
> Strong in the strength which God supplies
> Through His eternal Son.

Let us advance from being mere seekers after God's goods and become servants and soldiers enlisted for God's good.

But there is still a third stage in the developing relationship between Christ and his followers. At first seekers, then servants, and now in the farewell discourses recorded in the fifteenth chapter of John's Gospel, Christ says: "No longer do I call you servants, for the servant does not know what his master is doing; but I have called you friends, for all that I have heard from my Father I have made known to you." The third stage in the Christian's relationship with his Lord is that of *friendship*. To be a friend gives a warmth, an intimacy, an understanding, a confidence, which a servant does not enjoy.

Consider again Cicero's discussion, "On Friendship." He defines friendship as a complete accord on all things, joined with mutual good will and affection.[3]

Then let us hear how he developed one of his closest friendships, that with Scipio. He wrote that he was associated with him in business; lived with him in Rome and served abroad with him; and that they had similar tastes, pursuits, and sentiments, which was the true secret of friendship.

Suppose a Christian were to paraphrase those words of Cicero and apply them to his relationship with Jesus Christ. Listen: "With Christ I was associated in public and private business; with him I lived in my home city and served abroad; and between us there was the most complete harmony in our tastes, our pursuits, and our sentiments, which is the true secret of friendship."

[3] *Ibid.*, p. 14.

After describing friendship, Cicero makes the arresting assertion that it can exist only between good men. Then he goes on to define as "good" those whose actions and lives leave no doubt as to their honor, purity, equity and liberality; and those who are free from greed, lust, and violence and have the courage of their convictions.[4]

We may be inclined to challenge the statement that only good persons can be truly friends, for we recall the old saying about honor among thieves. We think of gangsters who are sometimes kind to crippled children and impoverished old neighbors.

But the bonds of friendship can prove dangerous between bad persons. Many a man has been led astray from the path of honesty by being loyal to a dishonest friend. When Hitler was organizing his Nazi groups, he said in substance: "You are my friends if you do what I command you." In loyalty to Hitler many a Nazi perpetrated atrocities on prisoners, especially on Jews. Bad persons can pervert the blessings of friendship.

Now are we not beginning to see why Jesus uttered the seemingly presumptuous statement, "You are my friends if you do what I command you"? We have to be obedient to Christ's commands of moral goodness if we are to enter into real friendship with him. Christ is always our friend, even when we are sinners, but only when we are good can we enter into that harmony of tastes, pursuits, and sentiments which Cicero said is the true secret of friendship.

Each of us might ask himself this searching question: "If I had a day to spend with Jesus, what would I talk about?" We are ever singing about our desire to be with him. But have we sufficiently learned to like what he liked and to be interested in his pursuits, to enjoy friendly associations with him? We like to sing the old hymn

> What a Friend we have in Jesus,
> All our sins and griefs to bear!

but do we stop to think what kind of a friend Jesus has in us?

[4] *Ibid.*

When we do advance from seeker to servant to friend in our relationship with Christ, what confidence and power and radiance come into our lives. We all know what it means to have someone with whom we can share our innermost thoughts, with whom we can unpack our hearts with words, knowing that he or she will sift the wheat from the chaff and make allowance for our moods.

Recently I called at the hospital on a man who lived pretty much alone. He told me that on the day I called he woke up free from pain for the first time in weeks. He said: "I wanted someone to share my feeling with." To have someone who shares our feelings of joy or pain, to have someone to love and be loved by—that makes life worth living.

Augustine Birrell, writing of the three Brontë sisters, daughters of an English rector, declared that only one had enough religion to give her pleasure. Some people have just enough awareness of God to make them feel uneasy when they do evil, but not enough fellowship with him to make them feel joyous when they do right. Horace Bushnell so lived and loved his way into understanding friendship with God that it was said even his dying was play to him.

The week end of Good Friday and Easter Sunday might be called the commencement season in Christ's school. His disciples, who began as seekers and continued as servants, had finished their course in faith as friends. After the resurrection they went forth as God's graduates.

Luke begins the Acts of the Apostles with a reference to his earlier book, the Gospel. He writes: "In the first book, O Theophilus, I have dealt with all that Jesus *began* to do and teach, until the day when he was taken up." In the Acts Luke continues the work of the living Christ through friends made vital and vocal by his indwelling presence.

The progress of physical science has made recent history a journey into wonder. As we watch our astronauts and our messages from Telstar, we exclaim, "What will man do next?" But do we ask, "What will God do next?" We seem to assume that the Creator has left us a universe of fixed laws and forces which man can explore and apply while God sits aloof immovable and unchanging. Paul

Hoon tells of seeing a list of questions submitted to high school youth for quick off-the-cuff answers. One was: "Do you think God understands radar?" The prevailing answer was, "No."

Perhaps our church vocabulary is partially responsible for the feeling that material science is outstripping divine activity. We say, "Jesus Christ, the same yesterday, today, and forever." And he is. But the force of electricity is the same yesterday, today, and forever, yet we are doing new things with electricity every day. The force of gravity is the same today as it was yesterday, but we have come a long way from Galileo to John Glenn. Similarly, though God in Christ is eternally the same in character, he can do ever new things with the spirits of men.

We should remember that, when a child becomes understandingly responsive to a father, the two together can accomplish what they could not do before. When we children of God graduate into true friendship with God we open infinite new possibilities of experience. Man can achieve wonders in the world of the spirit commensurate with those in the world of space.

INDEX OF SCRIPTURE REFERENCES

INDEX OF SCRIPTURE REFERENCES